T0148231

Can Two Walk Together

Willadean Logan

authorHOUSE®

AuthorHouse™
1663 Liberty Drive
Bloomington, IN 47403
www.authorhouse.com
Phone: 1-800-839-8640

Published by AuthorHouse   05/30/2012

ISBN: 978-1-4772-0989-9 (sc)
ISBN: 978-1-4772-0991-2 (e)

Library of Congress Control Number: 2012908959

Any people depicted in stock imagery provided by Thinkstock are models, and such images are being used for illustrative purposes only.
Certain stock imagery © Thinkstock.

This book is printed on acid-free paper.

Because of the dynamic nature of the Internet, any web addresses or links contained in this book may have changed since publication and may no longer be valid. The views expressed in this work are solely those of the author and do not necessarily reflect the views of the publisher, and the publisher hereby disclaims any responsibility for them.

memoir (65 years of their marriage)

Introduction

Many years, many miles, many memories have occurred since the last page of my previous book was written. "How My Parents Developed a Character" portrayed my years growing up until Keith and I started our journey together. Notice I didn't say that my growing up was completed. Or Keith's either. We always felt we grew up together, from my age 18 and his at 20 and onward.

Keith used to urge me to write another book of our lives together. My answer was that once I met him, my life just became a blur. Of course, that made his day. So no book was forthcoming then until now. If he is listening, this wait of many years will not surprise him. I trained him well to wait for me until . . . . whenever.

I should tell you that our twosome journey reached a fork in the road. My highway is continuing on. His branched off to a more complete life than I can fathom after he reached his destination marked "Heaven". You may wonder how I can be sure of that destination. More importantly, how Keith could be sure. That certainty can be yours, too. It's all in the instruction book for life, the Bible, written by the One who made the universe. This is just one sample promise: These things have I written unto you that believe on the name of the Son of God; that you may know that you have eternal life. 1 John 5:13a. The underlining is mine, wanting to emphasize that we CAN know where we are going.

That fork in the road showed up quickly in 2010 when Keith was 85 years old. He had been diagnosed 8 months earlier with non-Hodgkins lymphoma, and was told, following treatment, he was in remission. But only a few weeks later, a CTScan revealed five tumors in his brain. The One who determines the number of our days, was moving swiftly. I had to move along with Him, thus changing our walking together nearly 65 years to now walking alone; a new journey.

In order to pick up my story, I must take a giant step in reverse back to the attack on Pearl Harbor that plunged our country into World War II. The long fingers of the draft reached into every eligible young man's life. Keith was no exception. The fact that I thought he was exceptional carried no weight with the military. He was given a choice of branch of Service, and he chose Marines. However, he was determined ineligible when they discovered he was color blind—news to him. So his second choice was Seabees, a Construction Battalion (CB), a branch of the Navy. That proved to be a good choice. One of the immediate needs was to extend landing strips near Pearl Harbor to accommodate large bombers. This required a lot of cement work; a big job for the CB's. It was a skill Keith found useful later in life. I know—it was just tough luck on his part, that it took place in Hawaii. Family taunts included

"Why don't you trade in that Iowa blond who promised to wait for you, for a gorgeous brunette with a grass skirt?" I'm not saying there wasn't any rethinking on his part, but he did find his way back to Iowa clasping an honorable discharge dated Sept. 4, 1945.

Service to our country

He apparently had Iowa on his mind part of the time—remembering what he left back there. He loved to hunt sea shells in the ocean, and had polished some of these, and designed a necklace and earrings for me. He also had salvaged a piece of stainless steel from one of the Japanese bombed partially sunken ships (not restricted at that time) and designed and tooled a bracelet for me.

During his two years of service, he seized on to an opportunity to add a few shekels to the pitifully small wage the U. S. paid him. He washed and pressed uniforms, shirts, and bedding for other sailors who preferred to use their time for bar hopping and other night life activities. As "washerwoman" he saved $300 and bought a used car in Rhode Island, driving it home, taking two other buddies to their homes on the way. His arrival home was a happy reunion day for the two of us.

Two Became One

Following Keith's discharge, we began making our wedding plans. The invitations asked for their attendance at the Salem Friends Church for an evening ceremony. Rain fell all that day, but we didn't mind. How could drops of water falling from the sky possibly interrupt what we each felt was a divine plan for us to be together. I had expressed that in a verse. My sister, Marguerite, sang those words to the tune of "O Promise Me". I titled it:

∞ ∞ ∞ ∞

AS GOD HATH PLANNED

My darling, kindly take my trembling hand,
That both together, we might understand
The mysteries that life doth hold in store,
And whisper that you love me more and more.
Look in my eyes with yours so calm and sweet,
Thus giving courage, every fear to meet.
Close by your side, my dear, I'll always stand.
As God hath planned! As God hath planned!

The love that binds our hearts together now
Will deeper grow throughout the years somehow.
And as we promise to "love and obey"
We're thankful that God made for us this day.
Our hopes and dreams need never face defeat
Since joy and peace in Christ is so complete;
A love that's guided by an angel's hand.
As God hath planned! As God hath planned!

∞ ∞ ∞ ∞

Starting our journey

Following the ceremony, Keith used to say he thought he should repair the church floor where his nervous feet wore an indented place. I never knew if he was fidgety because he thought I might back out, OR that HE might, OR perhaps should! It WAS his last chance. It was best I never asked. It was also best we couldn't begin to know what the years ahead would hold. Quoting again from that instruction Book, planning a day at a time is sufficient.

This time of being presented as husband and wife brings up an important question. Can two walk together? Here is the situation. A strong willed female and a strong willed male ought to present enough of a discord to answer a definite "No" to the question. Add to that, different parents who have given us different gene makeup, different environment, different upbringing, both immature individuals and put them under the same roof and behold! Sweet harmony? Certainly not! Impossible! Only God could have thought up such a plan as marriage. Since the question is found in the Bible, book of Amos 3:3 it's important to note the question is followed by the word "except. "So there is an exception. "Can two walk together except they be agreed." That sounds better, but the pitfall remains—we each are strong willed. Agreed on what? Don't tell me what to agree on; I see it this way!

Even though prior to our marriage we each had confessed our sin nature to the Lord and asked Jesus to save us, and He did, we had not really submitted our wills to Him as we should. So we first of all, had to learn to "be agreed" with the Lord's plan for our lives. Just singing about it at our wedding

4

was not enough. Day by day, we first must agree with Him, the One who knows all things and direct our steps. Then to agree with each other was easy. Even though we stumbled along the way, there was always forgiveness and a chance to start again that allowed us to walk together for nearly 65 years. That last mile in our road together was precious beyond words, only because of agreeing first with the Lord's plan. The answer to the question "Can two walk together?" is a definite "Yes". Two can walk together because they are agreed first with the Lord.

It was a good thing Keith and I were in love with each other. We started life together with not much more than that to live on. Keith had saved enough to buy our first car; I had saved enough to buy a new wood-burning range and a small used table and two chairs. This and the bedroom set, waterfall style, I had purchased previously was all we needed??

Keith learned there was an opening for a farm hand in the Wayland, Iowa vicinity, working for Max Kauffman, the land owner. Keith applied and was hired. Thinking back to the large number of service men who were returning home due to the end of World War II, we were fortunate to have had an income, however small. Involved were long hours and hard work. It did include free rent of an old farm house with a chimney for a space heater. Of course we didn't have a space heater, but Keith's parents did. Years earlier when they had needed it, Keith had located one for the big sum of $1.00. Since they no longer needed it, gave it to us. It gobbled up wood relentlessly, but you could warm your body one side at a time, if you cuddled

5

close to its round belly. However, that amount of heat was not enough to prevent water freezing overnight in the wash basin in the next room. That is, if you had left well water in the basin. The house had no running water, no electricity. We dressed warm, and our new kitchen cook range helped to warm the kitchen. Some times when our car would not start in that cold Iowa winter, Keith walked the mile and a half or so to work. B-r-r-r!

Iowa is well known for hot summers following cold winters. This was no exception. So as the solar heat wore on causing the poison ivy to flourish in the fence rows, Max gave Keith the job of removing it. Keith knew he was highly allergic to poison ivy, and asked Max to please let him exchange work with the other hired hand, who was not sensitive to it, but Max refused. Following were these instructions—just roll up your sleeves and dig in; which he did. It was only a few days before the poison had overtaken Keith's system and he was hospitalized. The prolonged recovery meant he had worked less than half the days of the month. But since the cause was work related, we had no thought of not being paid for sick leave. The boss had other ideas, it became a lean month. It was easy after that to decide to look for other work if we could find it. Also by now, we had a third little mouth to feed in our household.

A Child—Our Heritage

The next year, a daughter had come to grace our home with her presence. What a growing up day that was for me. This warm little bundle was no make-believe doll, but a sweet, live baby who could love me back. She did not come with a "How To" book, so, if she could only have known how this was partially an experiment on our part, she would have been wise to seek safety elsewhere. Thankfully it was also a learning experience for us as we began to realize how much advice there is in Scripture about raising children. She did survive and became a beautiful, healthy little girl.

In seeking other work, Keith heard of Nick Roth, a tall, kindly gentleman who was making a way for himself and his family in the area, having burned out in Nebraska. He worked for a Mt. Pleasant attorney who owned farm land. The attorney had an acreage east of Prairie Gem that needed a worker. Nick, being the compassionate kind of fellow he was, wanted to help us get a better start. So we agreed to move to that house and work for Nick, who, in turn answered to the Attorney. Nick helped us to buy a cow for our own milk, and some chickens, and make a garden. He even offered to see if the attorney would help us get started on our own. But that was not to be. So we continued to work for Nick. He could see Keith was a hard worker. Nick was so generous on our behalf. He kept his eyes open for used machinery for Keith to buy. We were able to accumulate enough equipment to eventually rent an acreage ourselves south of Wayland. So we moved our meager belongings back there, and into a very nice house, newer than most. It provided electricity by means of a generator from many batteries in the basement; really elegant living for us. Though we had some electric appliances, we still used our kerosene refrigerator, however, because that is what we already had.

We farmed that acreage on our own as best we could. One event that I remember well was we had a field of wheat just ready to be harvested, when hail swept through and claimed the crop in a matter of minutes. Another startling incident was when we suddenly had no propane gas in a large tank that was partly full. A horse had stepped wrong that removed the cap letting all the gas escape. Some good memories were the peach trees and an apricot tree on the property. Canning that fruit was a joy.

We had neighbors north of us, through our field, down into a ravine and back up the other side, probably at least a half mile of tough walking. They befriended us, and we them, and walked to each other's house from time to time. The two big hills were a challenge to my very pregnant condition. But, undoubtedly the exercise was a good thing.

We attended a country church while living there. The Grabers phoned us one Sunday morning to see if we would go to their house for dinner after church, and we agreed. However, we hadn't taken a vote from the fourth member of our family, a daughter, who decided to make her appearance that Sunday morning. The Grabers considered this a valid reason to cancel. As I held our second warm little bundle, I realized she was like a Valentine, even if a little late.

Iowa may have cold winters and hot summers, but you haven't experienced it all until you see what a spring thaw can do to that rich, Iowa, stone free soil. The word bottomless comes to mind. That is what it was on the mud lane from our house to the main graveled road. Keith had brought our second daughter and I home from the hospital in Mt. Pleasant, and then took the car back out to the end of the lane to the graveled road, walking home. So when we needed groceries, or whatever, he either walked, or rode the horse out to the car. My memory may be exaggerating the length of time this occurred, but I thought it was 6 weeks before our two little ones and I could leave the house on a solid road. We got well acquainted. The older sister was intrigued with a doll that was not pretend.

The owners of our farm and house had been living in Florida, I think it was, and were planning to move back. So this meant they needed their house—another move for us. We were fortunate to have an opportunity to rent land again, north of Canaan Church near Mt. Union. I cannot recall who we rented from, and wonder if it was by way of Nick Roth again. Whether that is the case or not, I want to mention that many years later, our paths had not crossed for a long time. Keith learned that Nick was in the hospital, I think in Washington, Iowa, so he went to see him. That dear man had had to have a leg amputated, and he was pretty low in spirit. Keith came home from that visit, and said that the two of them just had simply cried together. Then many more years later, after we had lived in Missouri for a long time, a phone call revealed Nick's son had searched us out, and took time to phone us bringing us up to date. We were so blessed to have known that godly family, who lived what they believed.

A Move To Canaan

The acreage we moved to was rich Canaan Township soil, some of the richest in the country. The down side of that is that the road to our house was black gumbo. It is not yet known how deep that goes when the frost goes out. Keith bought an old Jeep, took the fenders off, so the black gum-like soil could wrap around and still keep going if the motor could pull it. You do learn to take Iowa's winters, spring thaws, and hot summers in stride. It is a great state.

We had neighbors who worked with us while haying or other big projects. Closest ones were Raymond and Florence. They attended First Baptist Church in Mt. Pleasant, and invited us to attend also. Even though it was quite a distance, we did start attending. That was a turning point in our lives as we sat under the excellent teaching of Pastor Stanley Andersen, whose wife was Elsie. We remained close friends of theirs until their deaths. Since then, their son and his wife have stayed in touch also. Stanley was a wonderful Bible teacher which both Keith and I soaked up like sponges. In addition to that was the strong Sunday School Class, "Truthseekers", taught by another great Bible teacher, Wanda Trueblood. The

Class became large with deep and lasting friendships formed. Only Heaven can reveal how great was the influence of that Church.

Wanda, front right

During our years of living there, neighbor Raymond would visit us. Our two girls loved those times. Once, the girls were on our front porch playing and could see Raymond out near the barn talking to Keith. Our second daughter began chattering her greeting to him. His usual teasing told her to dry up. So, next time he visited and she saw him near the barn, she called to him in her two year old voice and said "No, you dry up!", thus ruining her status as our shy one.

Part of that summer, Keith's younger brother lived with us. He had grown to be a strong young man and was helpful to Keith on the farm and to me, as well. My new pregnancy resulted in doctor's order to stay off my feet as much as possible, or risk losing the baby. I understood the importance of the order, but I didn't understand just how that was to be done. Our daughters were three and five, and Keith was busy with farm work. Some dear friends, also neighbors offered for me to bring our two young ones over to their house some of the days so I could rest on their couch. They already had two children as well, and busy farm work. I argued against their offer, but lost. It was such a kindness, and helpful. The threat subsided, and both families could go back to normal.

The custom thus far was to expect baby delivery on a Sunday, since both daughters were born on Sunday. So when Sunday in early October rolled around, even though my due date was not reached, I was feeling blah. We went after church to my parents' house. It was less miles to the hospital in Mt. Pleasant just in case that trip was needed. As the day wore on, we felt it best to enter the hospital. The girls stayed with my parents. The night hours continued on and on. I was ready to welcome whoever this was, if she/he would just appear. After the midnight hour opened up a new day (not Sunday) I should have suspected a new plan; an original plan. Something is different here. Whatever the plan, my ears were ready to hear the doctor's declaration, "It's a boy". And so it was that on that early Monday morning, our son entered our family. What a joy that was! He was a healthy boy. His attempt to greet us earlier should have clued us in to expect a lot of activity.

This inquisitive young man saw no need to crawl. A waste of time to learn, so just fold one leg partly under an ambitious body and scoot. And then suddenly graduate to climbing. No need to dust the tops of furniture, as he explored the tops of nearly every piece. As a new mother, while I was intrigued with how very different our two girls were, this was really new territory to experience the world of a boy. He did manage to mature, but probably only due to that ever present careful guidance of his two **more intelligent older sisters.** I, too, was the third sibling in my own family, so I understood all this guidance. How else would he and I have turned out so well!!

Our family of five attended church and Sunday school regularly, as well as enjoying an extra speaker occasionally. One that I recall gave each of us a real challenge to share the Christian message of joy and peace with those who have not heard. There were many people, including Keith and I, who responded publicly by going to the front, nearly filling the platform. Some may have responded as renewal of their faith in Christ. While it did mean that to me, it meant more. I truly saw the great need of missions, giving myself from that day on to missions, wherever that may take me. Day after day I mentally reviewed my commitment. It was genuine. But the reality of what was involved was very perplexing. How could I, a young wife, not only with family and farm duties, but financial obligations as well, responsibilities of three small children, and in need of my own further schooling be able to answer a call to missions? Had I made a mistake? Was my decision just a whim? One day the answer came. It could not have been clearer, not in audible words, but impressed deep in my heart: "Your mission field is your three children." And so it was. I began to see in a new way, the privilege given to me of molding three pliable, yet very diverse young lives.

Since the children's undivided time in my care was short before public school captured their time, I attempted to give them as much of a Biblical foundation as I could. The "tool" for that mission work was already in my house. My oldest sister had given us a Hurlbut's Story of the Bible, written for children. I decided to read it through to them before they started the years of public school. We were often challenged with schedules, but stuck with it as much as possible. They had favorite stories they liked to hear over and over. Favorite pictures, as well. It was a silent tool for learning things that were alright to do and not to do, as the Bible characters lived out their lives. During the last year of Keith's and my lives together as he battled cancer, he reviewed times we had together. He mentioned this activity I had with the children and wished he could have participated more in that area, but felt the pressure of so many daily work duties on the farm. That made me realize how often I, too, could get my priorities confused as to what is most important in life.

Keiwilla Ranch

Keith and I had been pursuing the possibility of purchasing our own farm. It was difficult to bring together affordable property, and the needed financing, along with a house for our family. Our son was now over two years old. And the girls needed to be in a good school district. This finally all came together with less than 300 acres of rolling crop/pasture land, an FHA (Farmers' Home Administration) loan, a livable two story house, and the Mt. Pleasant School District; a bold step forward for us in 1954. We placed an overhead entrance sign at the lane leading up to our house, calling it Keiwilla Ranch. I guess that looked like Indian language to some, but was actually a combination of our two names.

Combining nine years of adventure into a few sentences is not practical. So until our gigantic leap into the state of Missouri in 1963, I will condense it all mentioning some memorable times. Some medical situations: During milking time, Keith was stung by an unknown creature, resulting with his face immediately swelling until his eyes were shut. We headed for the doctor's office and he received a Penicillin shot. That was worse than the sting. Swelling was exaggerated, breathing labored, after which he was advised NEVER again to take Penicillin. The doctor gave him Benadryl capsules to carry with him in the event of another sting. A helpful solution except for the time he took two capsules instead of one. More was not better.

Keiwilla Ranch

While our children were having mild cases of mumps, we soon learned that apparently Keith had not had mumps as a child. So, he, too, was becoming puffed up. Medically, it is no light thing for a grown man to have mumps. All advice was to go to bed and stay there, or be prepared for dangerous complications. Good advice except he had sows that were pigging, and needed attention. I had children needing attention. His solution was he took a large scarf and tied it tightly around his jaws and over the top of his head, hoping to prevent the mumps from "going down", and continued to take care of our livestock. Between his "invention" and the blessing of our Heavenly Father, he survived without complications. I well remember the first Sunday he was able to attend church, our Pastor, Stanley Andersen met him at the door, with a smile, quoting a Bible verse: "When I became a man, I put away childish things."

One evening as I rushed to fix supper, I needed to use my electric mixer. For safety, I always kept it unplugged. So I asked our son, who was near the receptacle to please plug it in, which he did. Through the days, I had allowed him to use the bowl turntable to play on with his little cars, for a speedy "track". But this time, his childhood fingers had moved the switch to "on". Just as I was inserting the beaters the plug connection was made, which resulted with a truly "mixed up" little finger of my left hand. The mixer was on the floor, our son was crying, I was fainting, and Keith came to see what was happening underneath the now bloody towel wrapped around my hand. So Dr. Megorden again met our challenge, this time of piecing together, as best he could, the little finger jig-saw puzzle flesh. Even all these years has not erased the entire scar.

Our riding horse, Wink, was so useful for riding back to the pond to fish, checking on cows, or numerous other chores. But she had a problem. She was entirely too smart. This created a constant game to keep ahead of her antics. Our well was located on the top of a hill just west of our house with a water storage tank beside it. Underground piping brought gravity flow water into our house: a wonderful set-up to have running water for the first time in my life. However, it did not take "Water Pump 101" to teach Wink to turn the pump on and drink refreshing water from the spout. The fact that she had water available to drink, and the fact that she didn't bother to turn the switch back off, were no concern of hers. So she was seldom left unattended in that small orchard. But that was no big deterrent since the entrance latch on the gate, which was difficult for the children to maneuver, for her was a piece of cake. No! More like a lump of sugar to Wink.

So the contest went on. If they give Grammy Awards to talented horses, she would definitely win. The "award" I had in my mind was more like a life sentence without parole; especially following her next episode. The previous owner of our farm had planted a fruit orchard. The peach trees had yielded that day an abundant two bushels of peaches, which we had picked and placed under a shade tree just outside the house for overnight, since the house temperature was too hot for them. The next morning, I couldn't believe my eyes! Those beautiful peaches were mashed, slobbered over, some with seeds spit out on top of them, a grand mess! Do you think I wondered how this could have happened?? No DNA needed for a four-legged culprit nearby. O.K., so she was tall and beautiful, but not to me that day. She was my enemy! She got no sympathy from me, either, for a very obvious belly ache. While her punishment wasn't prison without parole, she did have to be tethered to the stall in the barn.

If you have never raised sheep, you may not fully comprehend their helplessness and stupidity. It is not a mistake that Scripture often compares us, God's children to sheep. Wandering around, doing whatever the one ahead of us is doing, going down the side of a cliff to get a blade of grass, forever having to be rescued.

This became one of the duties of the shepherd, which, in Bible times and even now in the East have not varied much. The flocks are still led out of the fold in the morning by the shepherd as he calls to them. They know his voice and they follow him. They will not follow the voice of a stranger. John 10 tells us of the Good Shepherd, as Jesus calls himself. Those of us who follow him are grateful that he goes before us. He does not drive us, he leads us. Psalm 23 tells us he leads us into green pasture and beside still waters. Sheep will not drink from turbulent water. He provides still water. Our Good Shepherd provides for us so abundantly, and frees us, too, from many disturbances. We need not be disturbed even as we face death, because he is with us. He is simply taking us home to the place he has prepared for us. He would welcome you to his fold as you answer the call of his voice.

On Keiwilla Ranch, the choice that Keith and I made to raise sheep was good for the type of land we had: hills, brushy places and such. AND, as our children will testify to the fact, a sheep's offspring, little wooly lambs, are adorable as well as entertaining. Jumping around stiff-legged on a small hill, playing "king of the mountain" and other antics.

One day, we noticed several of our sheep were ill, some even dying, and we could not discover the reason. Keith determined to continue checking, until one day he discovered their hoofs were sore. Above the solid part of the hoof, infections were taking over, and with some gentle probing found white maggots that feast on infection had invaded that soft tissue. Then as the sheep would lie down to rest with their legs folded under them, the maggots would eat into their bellies and chests. Thus, death was not far away. During all that morning Keith took over the nasty job of extracting the maggots, sheep by sheep, and treating the wounded flesh. I was not aware of his project. When he came into the house for lunch, I had a bowl of cooked white rice on the table, the worst possible choice. Just the sight of it turned his stomach and removed any hunger he probably felt. It was a long time before he could again eat one of his favorite dishes, creamed rice.

During the nine years of living on Keiwilla Ranch, and many wonderful experiences to recall, there is also a very sad one. We had become friends with neighbors Ivan and June Byczek and their three children, similar in age to our three. In addition to June's many duties of raising a family, a productive garden, and helping with the farm work, she was a talented piano player. She gave piano lessons to our daughters. One afternoon, the message came to me that there had been an accident on the Byczek farm. Keith was not home at the time, but I left a note to tell him where I had gone. The rushed schedule of spring plowing and planting was upon us. June and Ivan both were on tractors plowing in the same field, but in different sections. Ivan did not see her tractor showing up at the expected time. On investigating, apparently her tractor had hit a hole or barrier of some kind that caused her to fall beneath it, and be dragged by the plow. I cannot think of any site in the world worse for Ivan to discover.

Keith came to the Byczek home as soon as he got back to our house. We had no words for each other, only to hold each other and cry. I cannot fathom the depth of sorrow, the mental anguish, and the adjustments of each member of this dear family. And that continued for months to come, never to be the same again. The mother of Ivan and the mother of June, both with aging and questionable health themselves, helped with necessary household duties, trying to obtain a semblance of family normalcy. Keith and I did what we could, also. Sometimes, I attempted to lend a motherly ear or a hug to their middle child. Ivan was so overwhelmed with it all, attempting to know how to wipe away a tear, fix a pony tail, or just keep the laundry done and the groceries bought. My heart just ached for the whole family. Their youngest was not yet of school age. The oldest, was near the age of our oldest, and they, later, did date some. But that terrible day of May 11, 1960 forever changed our family as well as theirs.

To complicate the issue even further, Ivan and June were like any number of other young couples, not preparing a will that would help protect themselves and minor children, and prevent the State from making the decisions. This was not even on their agenda, or ours. We were young. There is tomorrow. Also having a family photo taken, we had not done that either. You can be certain that both these two items were accomplished by us as soon as we possibly could. During the depths of sorrow, the helpful lesson we learned, when it is late, It may be too late. Do it today.

After Ivan's long time of mourning and trying to be a Dad and Mother to three children, and keep up with farming and loneliness, there came a time when he was able to consider dating. I was working in Mt. Pleasant at the time as bookkeeper in a hardware/dry goods store called Brown Lynch Scott. A co-worker, Velma, mentioned to me one day, she had been alone all her life, caring for her aging parents, and was interested in pursuing a new life for herself. I heard my matchmaker button click into gear. But, be realistic, I told myself. This lady surely defines the "new life for herself" as a life of romance and male companionship. This "offer" might well include that, but there is the small detail of raising three children, with many foreseeable complications as well as many unforeseen ones. Her resume' would show "no experience" on that page.

There was the Byczek household, and Velma's household engrossed in much thought as the subject was sometimes considered. Conclusion was the adage "Nothing ventured, nothing gained." Velma invited Ivan to come to her house to meet her. Keith and I would introduce them, but arrive in separate cars, so we could dismiss ourselves. Ivan was so nervous, understandably. Velma probably was also. So after meeting in her house, for a few minutes of chit-chat, Keith asked Velma to bring him his coat and hat so we could leave. AND Ivan asked for his, as well. This was NOT the plan. But being a dutiful hostess, she brought Ivan's as well. I was confused. Had Ivan seen all he wanted? Velma was perplexed by such a short meeting. But Keith saved the day by suggesting to Ivan that we would leave, and then he could leave later when he was ready. So an awkward, embarrassing situation was snatched away and replaced with laughter. The evening's acquaintance for those two was followed by many others including getting acquainted with the children. Velma did become Velma Byczek and took on the gigantic task to add to her resume': "experience raising children."

Additional Income

The type of farm loan we had was an attempt by the government to arrange a farm purchase that was self supporting, and Keith, as the principal farmer was not allowed to work off the farm. In theory, this was ideal. But weather, and circumstances, and other incidents are almost never ideal. So when milk cows were purchased at an auction to increase our herd, there was no way Keith could have known that the reason the farmer was selling them was because they had Bangs Disease. It causes them to abort their calves. This does not affect the meat from being used, only the reproductive organs. But the meat packing plants used this as a reason to stamp the cow "unfit for human consumption." You can imagine what price would be gained from the mandatory sale. So when the problem surfaced soon after we purchased them, we were left with no recourse. No laws made it illegal to sell them. Thankfully, that is no longer true. So while Keith could not work off the farm, I could, and started working at the Geigy Chemical Plant in Lockridge. Wayne Rohrman was the plant manager, and attended our church. He was gracious to give me work, in the plant, bottling liquids, or measuring out dry chemicals to package and occasional secretarial work. My family did not like how I smelled after arriving home, but they did not mind an extra paycheck. The plant eventually relocated to a larger city. I became bookkeeper at Lockridge Lumber Yard, and later traveled part-time also to the Wayland branch of the same company.

Central States Insurance Company in Mt. Pleasant hired about 22 workers, and I was able to get full time work there. This was in the early days of computer, when it took a large room with controlled climate to house one computer machine. It used the key-punch/verify method. Mostly, I ran a verify machine, checking to see if the key puncher had made any errors. I really liked that job. There were times I also took dictation, typed and did filing. I was fortunate to get a good job, although the employees were not without their power struggles.

Two good friends, who also attended Church, were starting a Farm Bureau Insurance Office combined with the County Extension Office. Each of them was the head of each office, so the secretary they were looking to hire would be answering to both bosses. They offered it to me, and I took it. It was quite different from work I had done, and working for two bosses sometimes got complicated. But for the most part was enjoyable.

Later on, I worked part-time as secretary to Pastor Troxel, in our new church building. He and others had sacrificed a lot to complete that lovely building, which is still beautiful today.

Mt. Pleasant First Baptist Church

That work was very fulfilling to me. Many things were told in confidence to the Pastor. While I was not told of these things, I gained insights into the life of a Pastor and his faithful wife, Rosemary. Not only was she helpful to teach me her wisdom on how to stretch a dollar within the household, but also to realize the depth of her partnership with Jim was a beautiful thing, yet unknown to most as she remained in the background. For instance, no matter how late the hour of his return home from meetings, travelling, or counseling, which he did so well, Rosemary was waiting up for him with her sweet presence, no doubt thoroughly exhausted herself. Her encouragement meant so much to him. It was not unusual the next day, after catching a few short hours of sleep, for him to arrive later than usual to the office, thus to face a critical parishioner, not knowing the whole story. Remarks like "I wish I had a cushy job that allowed me to come in at 10:00". But it was always met with a smile not being able to justify himself due to the confidential work of perhaps saving a marriage, or other private concern. It could have been meeting with two homosexuals who needed God's message; all of which may have lasted to the near dawn hours before he could get to his bed.

A situation that opened my eyes was the beggars who often showed up at the church office. You could not assess that label to them by appearance. Sometimes one would arrive in a junk-like car with a back seat full of children. The man driver would pull up so the woman could come inside with a plea for assistance, "desperately needing money". The need may be legitimate, or it may be rehearsed and reused elsewhere. We had no divine insight to tell the difference. Some of the stories could really pull your heart strings. Previous experience had caused the church to implement a workable plan, starting with never, never giving money that might be used for food and/or gas. But also might go to a long substance abuse. So, the plan was an agreement with a gas station for them to put in a certain amount of gas; and with a restaurant that allowed a set amount of food per person. It was a compassionate gift.

As parents, we were so grateful that each of our three children had come to realize their need to be forgiven of sin. Being in a Christian home as well as constantly attending a Christ centered church did not make them Christians. Each one had to make that decision for himself, even as Keith and I each had done years before. Each one followed the Lord's instruction to make that choice public by being baptized. The joy that comes from walking in obedience to the Scripture is hard to define, unless you have experienced it.

The Greener Grass Of Missouri

Keith and I had lived our entire lives in Iowa, and had passed the 18th year of our marriage. We had friends who had moved to southwest Missouri with reports of milder winters, cheaper land and other allurements. After we found a property to buy near Verona, Missouri, we proceeded to sell our Iowa farm. That was not without its pitfalls, having moved temporarily to a rented house near Monett, MO. until the final closing took place. And it didn't take place, after the potential buyer experienced a crop loss due to heavy rains, and had to forfeit. We went back to our Iowa farm and eventually procured a buyer. The big move to Missouri did occur in winter, 1963: a dog, cats, chickens, hogs, cattle, horses, two cars, a cattle truck, a moving truck (our own), furniture, oh yes, and children. The day our first procession left Iowa, morning temperature was 20 degrees below zero, and when we arrived it was above freezing. We thought we may have made a wrong turn to Florida. We soon learned that not all Missouri winters are mild, however.

There were Iowa folks who had known us since childhood, and other acquaintances that just shook their heads, thinking our family surely must have taken leave of its senses to make such a move. That included our very caring family doctor, Dr.

30

Megorden, who had delivered our last two children. Quote: "Why would you want to take your precious family to that illiterate state?" Actually, Missouri had purposely cultivated an image of barefoot hillbillies, and corncob pipe smokers tending their stills; all for tourist entertainment. In some ways, we found its literary standards to be equal to or above Iowa's.

Because the farm house situated on the land we bought needed repair and updating, we moved into another farm house and cared for the owner's cattle in lieu of the rent while our house was being worked on. Keith's Dad and Mom came from Iowa and helped Keith and me with the work. It seemed to take a long time, but we got it in a livable condition and moved in. We continued to eat plaster dust even after that with further work. A cabinet builder from the area built some nice kitchen cabinets, and we enjoyed a large sink with running water. He also built nice cabinets in our newly made bathroom. We also enclosed the front porch as an extra family room with fireplace, and an adjoining wood-box that we filled from outdoors. Real up town! We did enjoy our comfortable home.

I found some part-time work as secretary to the head of the Chamber of Commerce in Monett. Later, I worked across the street for Les Mason Insurance and Loans for more hours a week. Soon after I changed jobs, the Chamber of Commerce man was answering his phone at work, and collapsed and died. It was a shock to all who knew him.

My work for Mr. Mason was Monday-Friday and till noon on Saturdays. I liked my work there, but on Saturdays, I so needed to be at home catching up. The kids were all a big help and we managed. Mr. Mason told me one day that he planned to double my wages. He was a man who enjoyed jokes and life as a whole, so I knew he might increase my wage, but not double it. The next week he had my check written out, folded it, and handed it to me saying "Doubled, just like I promised". I enjoyed the joke, but found it didn't buy any more groceries than usual.

Clouds Filled With Blessings

On the Saturday before Labor Day, our family was geared up for a reunion at our Missouri home. Friends from First Baptist Church of Mt. Pleasant, Iowa; Glenn and Jeanette, Frank and Virginia, along with some who lived nearby Gifford and Jerry and former pastor, Stanley Andersen and his wife Elsie, all living near Table Rock Lake. Keith and I were so excited to have them come. This was one Saturday morning that I surely needed to be home from my job, but could not. The children each had their jobs assigned, preparing sleeping arrangements, and some cleaning. Keith was getting the cattle into the lot to spray them for flies. However, no one assigned the riding horse (not Wink) his duties. The usually very congenial horse, for an unknown reason, began to buck before Keith was completely in the saddle, pitching him onto the nearest rock. He continued to get the cattle into the lot, sprayed them and then limped into the house. Our oldest daughter learned what had happened. Though his pant legs were wider than his jeans would have been she saw that his leg was already swollen tight and told him he should go to the doctor. But, of course, this tight work pant leg was not on his tight schedule so "there was no time for that." But the few minutes Keith rested, Our daughter noticed the urgency increased. She was not experienced in driving our 1959 stick shift Rambler, but had done it some. So, he agreed to let her take him. It was with fear and trembling that she drove him to the doctor's office in Aurora.

He limped into Dr. Morrison's office, and they could see he needed help. So took him back and laid him on a table. By then it was almost impossible to get his trousers off, but did get it done to expose his gigantic leg and thigh. The doctor told Keith he must have severed a main blood vessel and gave him a shot, ordering him to go to the hospital. He insisted he "did not have time", but knew down deep he had no choice.

Our daughter got him into the back seat of the car. He was in such pain, holding his left arm against his chest, and then he let out a loud groan. And she didn't know what was happening. She was so shook up by this time, ran back into the office and asked for someone to help her take him to the hospital, even asking the nurse to go. She told our daughter she could not leave the doctor's office, but since I was still at work, and the need was so great, she did go and drove the car.

Arriving at the hospital, his huge leg had become wedged between the front and back seat, and would not bend enough for them to get him out. So as they forced him out, our daughter said he was pleading with her to please not let them hurt him so. This was about too much for her to take. An EKG was attached and the doctor's expression of alarm was being noticed. He later called our daughter out into the hall, and said "Your Dad has had a heart attack. He will need much bed rest, and should not be told of the heart condition." That was his diagnosis and solution, not unusual for that time period. However, today, much different methods would have been used. If our memories serve us right he was hospitalized 21 days, and certainly did learn of the diagnosis from visitors prior to that. Following dismissal, he still needed a lot of rest, and limped on that leg for a long time. A very interesting sideline is that following lab work and tests for surgery, done in later years, each of those doctors reported that there was no evidence Keith had a heart attack at any time in his life. So what did occur, we really don't know.

Meanwhile, I still had my plans for the "reunion". When I arrived home from my work, ready to pitch in to help the family with any loose ends, I had no idea how "loose" they really were. I could scarcely absorb all the events of the morning, perplexed as to which way to turn. Reunion or not, I went immediately to the hospital, praying for guidance. As I recall, I stayed the night and the next day, the children went to church with a neighbor.

All four reunion couples arrived that same afternoon, without my presence. The kids did a great job, as far as I know, of greeting them, explaining the situation, settling them in to sleeping quarters, etc. Pastor Stan and Elsie came to the hospital immediately upon arrival, and I went home for a break. It was so good to see our old friends, even though the circumstance was not a cordial welcome for them. They all stayed overnight on Saturday and then headed back toward home, earlier than planned.

No need to have just one major issue when you can have two. Our daughter was almost ready to leave for John Brown University, enrolling for her freshman year. My sister Dorothy and Herb Payne from Mt.Pleasant were bringing their son, Leonard to enroll; daughter Linette came also. I think their other son, Lewis was still in school, so did not come. Also they brought Dora, my Mother. So, all that crew, and belongings—a big load—headed out for Siloam Springs, AR. Our daughter remembers arriving at the school. While the Paynes were getting Leonard settled into his room, my 65 year old Mother helped her to get moved into her room. I felt I was only half doing my duties not taking my daughter to college. Other times, I felt I was doing double duty, working in town, helping our two younger children feed the many hogs and doing other farm chores, and spending time at the hospital.

Why not throw in one more major event for good measure! One of the mornings, just after our two kids boarded the school bus headed west, a neighbor's phone call came to me that the bus was in an accident at the first corner west of our house and several were being taken to the hospital. For some reason, the bus driver had pulled out into the intersection from his stop sign into the path of another car. The driver was injured, and the kids, were shook up and bruised, but none seriously, thankfully. After I got the message that our kids were OK and going to school, it was time for me to go to my job. I probably did not give it my best that day.

Keith was glad to get back home from the hospital though he walked only with crutches, so it was slow going for him. A former acquaintance, also from Mt. Pleasant moved into the area prior to us. He came to visit Keith. Realizing recuperation was going to be long he mentioned that the United Farm Real Estate Agent for the area was quitting, and wondered if Keith might be interested in a less strenuous line of work than farming. That seemed to shine a bright light at the end of Keith's tunnel, and he made the contact with Forest King, District Manager for United Farm Agency.

Qualification for a real estate salesman license under the National United Farm Agency was fairly lenient at that time. So he studied, took the test and passed. He remembered (and reminded me occasionally) of my words of "encouragement" regarding his career change. My quote was "You can't sell real estate." Well, I have eaten crow before. Though it's not tasty, my reply after this reminder was "What are good wives for?" Truth be known, I was proud of his many accomplishments, as he seemed to have a sense about the value of land, and how to present it to a prospective buyer.

He started under a broker, in a Verona office. After a time of that, he felt like he wanted to be more serious about the business at hand and started up his own United Farm Agency office on south Elliott in Aurora, still being a salesman under the National Agency. Elliott Street was also Hwy. 39, and was being torn up and resurfaced, making it difficult for traffic to come to his office, but he kept busy listing and sold some properties, as well. He soon needed help and took on some salesmen. This was not as satisfactory as he had hoped. So we made the decision that it was best for me to give notice to quit my job with Les Mason and come help him with office work so he could be free to list and sell. This worked out fine for a while when later both of us became real estate brokers.

One of Keith's listings was for a nice house across the street from our east side small office. The Catons had moved here from CA. and had built the home with the best of materials. They wanted to move back and urged Keith to find a buyer. Since that didn't happen as quickly as they liked, Mr. Caton asked Keith to buy it. This was in 1966. Keith told him we had just purchased our farm acreage in 1963, had house remodeling expenses, and surely didn't need another house. Mr. Caton insisted and finally said "Just make me an offer." Again Keith argued and said that if he did he would embarrass Mr. Caton as well as himself. But Keith began to consider the possibility. We could move our office into the house without having the existing office-rent, could also get rent from the farm house, that would become vacant, and our son could change to the better school system of Aurora, so reluctantly he offered $15,500, and felt sure the owner would not take such a loss on the nearly new house. But he did! We considered this purchase to be a brief time of insanity on our part, but we soon realized it was one of the best decisions we ever made. The location was excellent for a real estate office and we enjoyed it for years. We dubbed it the pink house. In much later year when it again became a real estate office, the color of the paint was changed—no longer the pink house.

The one car garage made up the north end of our new home, so we adjusted it to become our office. This was an advantage to me, also, to be able to get house duties done in between office duties. Our daughters worked for us, each needing to earn finances for college, so a good location for them, too. Then there was another "helper", perhaps a bit dubious.

It seemed impossible for our cat lover daughter to be purr-less and fur-less for any length of time. The previous cats she had claimed were all needed out on the farm. But one day, she saw an ad in the paper for a house broken, neutered Siamese cat needing a home. She needed to check it out. She learned that the older owner of the cat had both a canary AND a cat. One or the other had to go. The canary was the survivor, the cat was voted off. She was told that mostly what he liked to eat was oyster soup. So as our daughter presented her plan to us to adopt the cat it became our decision of yes or no to give him a home. One part was easy. If it was yes, he would either experience a serious diet change or go hungry a lot. We did vote yes, learning later he surely was a questionable helper. Hence, Clarence, the Siamese cat came to our home. Our home was never the same again. He immediately appointed himself as the extra office helper already mentioned: the office doorbell rings, Clarence springs into action, checks out each customer, and if suitable, after customer sits down; Clarence does, too, on customer's lap. He was a big hit with the kids; not so much with adults. I probably should have titled one chapter "Clarence", but instead, will only report some of his antics. He would have loved to be known as an ideal cat, and worked hard at covering up evidence that proved otherwise. For instance, "I would never get up on the kitchen table even though it gave a good lookout thru the pulled drapes to see when the family car was returning home." The fact that beady eyes glared thru the window was no proof, because it just takes a quick dash to jump down and become curled up in a sleeping ball in big chair in the living room.

Clarence

Evidence #2: "I get lonesome when left alone for longer than I want, but I don't make a big issue of it and demand attention. Can I help it if the big lounge chair is tipped back into recliner notch and a few pictures behind the chair are on the floor? We could have had an earthquake. You weren't here, so you don't know."

Evidence #3, #4 & #5: "I happen to like eating garments, blankets, even a sweater, now and then. Well, not the whole thing; just a hole or two in a crucial place. Let the record show that you were told that I eat oyster soup, and I have not had one bowl since arriving here." Case dismissed.

One time we were gone overnight and our middle daughter was in charge of the cat. She and her husband knew where there was an abundance of black walnuts. Picking these up would provide a few spending coins for their income. So, as a favor to Clarence, they took him along for outdoor exercise. When it was time to return home, Clarence was nowhere to be found. They looked in the trees, under the car, calling and calling, which he usually responds to. It was nearly dark, and they decided they had lost him and started the car for home. Suddenly a sleepy, "innocent" faced cat was near the car wanting in. He must have been sleeping on the warm motor, and remember, he will wake up when HE is ready.

This next event should have sent him up to the Big House, but, on the witness stand, he was able as usual to turn it around to being my fault. We had to be out of town for an extended time, and our son-in-law was willing to come in to feed him and empty his litter pan. But Clarence did have a regular routine of going into the back yard each day for relaxation, and would come to the door to be let back in. I didn't feel our cat-sitter should be saddled with that consuming of his time. My only intention was to make a happy cat, so I hit on a marvelous plan only for his good. In our bathroom was a service door to access the plumbing. It also had a floor hole that accessed the crawl space under our house. So my plan was for Keith to fix a slanting board from the bathroom service door down to the crawl space, and hence outside, making it a self-service for Clarence's daily exercise routine. So Keith made the ramp, covering it with carpet for good traction and we had Clarence use it for the few days before we were to leave. It worked great. I was pleased.

When we returned home, we got our son-in-law's report. One of the days when he came to the house, the house was in disarray: floor lamp upset, chairs rearranged, the lounge chair tipped back, (probably another earthquake), pictures off the wall, large balls of fur and worse under the beds and elsewhere. It must have been some party. We had no idea other feline friends (??) would be invited. That was the end of my terrific invention of the ramp, and the end of Clarence's daily exercise till we got home. So, if you were on the jury, whose fault would this have been? You've heard of a hung jury. I'm thinking more of a hung cat.

But he remained a guest/boss in our household. After both girls were gone to college, our son and Clarence became buddies. Well, sort of; lots of skirmishes as well as sleeping on the human's back when he would lie on his stomach to watch TV. Then after he went away to college, it was just Clarence and us. We didn't need the responsibility. We had an offer to give him a home in the country, so we gave him to them. Later, our college son accused us of maybe even giving away one of our kids. Hmm! I hadn't thought of that.

Real Estate business

Keith and I had enjoyed several busy years in the real estate business. While there were advantages to having the office in our home, there was a down side to it, as well. One was that customers sometimes felt free to come to our office after hours, and on weekends or holidays, knowing that if there was no response to the office doorbell, there was always the doorbell at the front door of our house. We did not begrudge the fact that sometimes the result was a sale that another office missed out on for being closed. One example was a customer who interrupted our family meal on Christmas Day. I felt this was nearly unforgiveable. But Keith got up and ended up selling a sizeable chicken farm. See, I told you he couldn't sell real estate.

It became increasingly more difficult as our business increased, to maintain any regular attendance at Sunday-School and Church. The secret was in getting away before their arrival. For a while Keith taught a class of junior age boys, and I taught a class of sophomore girls. But we often had to cancel, and we hated that part of not being dependable. We began feeling the need of a respite. We learned of a couple who were retired from real estate, and were willing to run our office for a time so we could be gone. This was a great help to us though a bit difficult for them to fit in to previous agendas.

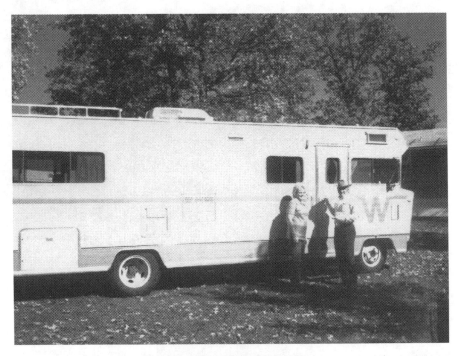

Heading for Alaska

We began arranging a trip to Alaska in our Winnebago motor home. As time drew near for our departure, there came the shocking news of our daughter's best friend's sudden disappearance. The life changing event for that family began when she apparently was taken from her home, yet leaving her young son. There were and still are many unanswered questions. We had hoped this sad situation would soon be solved, but that was not to be.

So after a few days, Keith and I did journey north toward the Alaska destination in our motor home. The trip could be described as enjoyable, educational, adventurous, and, at times a trip of endurance, with many graveled roads yet at that time. This was particularly true in the Northwest Territories and the Yukon. It was not unusual that sometimes our day's travel only covered a few miles traveling in deep ruts carved out in the rock covered roads. Even blacktop portions throughout Alaska were rough due to frost heaves, since frost does not ever completely leave some sections of Alaska. Little wonder, then that Alaska has over 5,000 glaciers, one of which is larger than the country of Switzerland. We were privileged to have so many experiences during the three months we were gone.

One privilege was toward the end of September when fall arrives early in that north land, we decided to book a portion of our return trip on a ferry called the Matanuska. This 352 foot ship, owned and operated by the Merchant Marines had a crew of 46. It has a basement car deck. As we were in line to get on board, Keith and Laddie were first in line with our motor home. I drove on later in line with our car. This was the final trip for the season, as inlet waters would soon freeze preventing passage. We learned that all the sleeping rooms had been booked, but passengers could still board and stay on the observation lounge and try to sleep in the chairs. We slept very little among the many passengers as we glided along. The observation deck allowed very little viewing due to fog, rain and just gloom in general. We covered about 500 miles at a speed of what would compare to 20 MPH for a total of almost 48 hours. So when we docked at Prince Rupert and unloaded the vehicles, we soon found a place to park, took a hot shower, and went to bed to get rested from a couple nearly sleepless nights.

I mentioned Laddie in the motor home with Keith for the ferry ride. He had made the long trip from Iowa to Missouri, and later the even longer trip to Alaska. He was a good traveler. Years earlier when we moved from our cattle/hog farm to the "pink house", Laddie had to adapt from acres to a city lot. He seemed to have an inner desire to still be on our team, though the rules had changed. Like Clarence, he enjoyed our real estate customers. I don't mean barking; he didn't do that. I mean hearing a car drive up, and walking to wait for the vehicle door to open, then sit with an extended paw to "shake"; pretty hard to resist a welcome like that. Our postman and he became real buddies, always with the paw shake.

Laddie

Laddie was content, mostly, with his smaller space. I guess his "greener grass syndrome" kicked in later, as we would notice sometimes seeing him across the street at the veterinarian's office. He had never ventured to cross the busy Highway 39, so how could he possibly be over there? Keith would call loudly to him to get back home. And in a few minutes, he did. Now the puzzle had doubled. He was not seen crossing the highway back home, so how did he do that? Eventually he was caught, shall we say red-handed? Our lot sloped quite a lot beyond its south border, to a small stream that ran in wet weather. We had paid no attention to a large concrete culvert under the highway for larger amounts of water flow—a perfect subway for a curious dog to check out the neighbor vet's most recent customers. Our neighborhood vet was gracious about these unexpected visits, but we still did our best to break him of this habit.

During real estate years, we had purchased land in northern Minnesota when a United Farm Agent there would find a good buy for us, so we made occasional trips there. Laddie would hop right in the R V lie down under dinette table, not needing attention until we stopped. But Laddie was getting old and had a lot of arthritis hardly able to get into the motor home anymore. One trip to Minnesota, he did not make it back home. So, his grave is under a tree on a farm we owned there.

April

April's first day was on Sunday. Keith and I were in a Sunday School Class when the Superintendent called us out, asking us to follow him to the Pastor's Office. We could not imagine why, but did so. The Pastor asked us to be seated and then relayed to us the sad news he had been given to tell us. Keith's brother, Billy, in Nevada had chosen to end his life. This was not something that could be absorbed instantly. We sat in shock and then decided to go home from church, attempting to clarify our plan from there. This we did in zombie-like fashion, arranging a flight to Nevada to be with the family and to attend the funeral. We changed planes in Denver, and met Keith's other brother as he flew in from Iowa. Our flight took us to Reno where we were met by a driver in a van who drove us northeast up to Winnemuca, still a lengthy ride, but the best arrangements to get there. Our stay with the family and the funeral took place over a few days, and was stressful to us as well as the rest of family. It all seemed a perplexing mystery with unanswered questions.

Coming back home, Keith and I and our two nieces flew in a small 6 passenger plane over mountains, and back into Reno for the main flight. His younger brother had decided to stay on

49

at the house for a while. Keith and I were drained emotionally and very glad to get back home to Missouri. My father, Dewey, in southeast Iowa, had been fighting colon cancer, and his condition was weakening. So, as soon as we could arrange it, Keith and I drove to Mt. Pleasant to see him and be a support to my Mother. He was beginning to lose touch with reality, and was hard for Mother to handle physically when he would fall or need other assistance. He had insisted previously to remain at home for his last days, but we helped Mother to arrange for an ambulance to come take him to the hospital in Mt. Pleasant. As he was loaded into the ambulance, I can still hear his words of disappointment in all of us: "You tricked me." As tough as that was, it was the correct decision to help my Mother, as we were leaving to go back to Missouri. Being home just a few days, we got the message that my father had died in the hospital on April 22. So drove back to Iowa for the April 25 funeral. While there, our daughter and son in law back home had a child on April 24. Next day after the funeral, we drove from Iowa to Missouri, visited briefly our new grandson in Aurora, threw a few clothes together and early next morning, left to drive to Shreveport, Louisiana where our son and wife, were living. Our son was graduating from LeTourneau College the next day in Longview, Texas. Mid-morning of the 28th, we got the news that our son in law's 16 year old brother, was killed on Highway 39 south of Aurora as he rode his bicycle. Next day we headed for home again in time to stay the following day with the new grandbaby while his parents went to the funeral.

In the event you might have gotten covered up in the frenzy of the month, our 1973 itinerary was:

April 1, Keith's brother died

April 2 Logan's to Nevada

April 3-9 Logan's with family in Nevada, then fly home

April 11 Logan's drove to Mt. Pleasant, Iowa

April 14 Arrange to hospitalize my father, drove to Missouri home

April 22 My father died

April 23 Logan's drove back to Iowa

April 24 Baby grandson born, Aurora, Missouri

April 25 Funeral for my father in Iowa

April 26 Logan's drove back to Missouri home, visit new grand baby

April 27 Logan's drove to Shreveport, Louisiana

April 27 Son graduated LeTourneau College, Longview, Texas

April 28 Son in law's brother killed in bicycle accident

April 29 Logan's drove from Shreveport to Missouri home

April 30 Funeral; Logan's stay with new grand baby

From that time to this, we Logan's have never had a comparable month of activities, and may that ever be true. Our real estate office still located in our home, did not have many sales that month.

Need I say Keith and I were shaken to the core following this month that included three deaths, one birth, and one college graduation? This covered over 12,000 miles, in five states, to Iowa two times and returning back to MO. four different times.

We weren't always sure if we were coming or going. We didn't have a lot of time to contemplate and be grateful for the firm foundation we each were fastened to, but knew for certain that "underneath were the everlasting arms." What a blessing!

Journeying On

Just a little over a month later, we were approached with an opportunity to sell our house with the office and equipment pertaining to the real estate business. The opportunity came at a time when we were weary, not just from the month of April, but the nine preceding years of real estate. I realize many have been in the business much longer than that, but probably all would agree that it is a rigorous business, one that is with you 24/7. However, we truly had numerous benefits from it, for which we are grateful.

We did sell the house and equipment and moved into a house south of Marionville on 10 acres. We had actually sold that property previously to a client in Minnesota who had gotten into a legal battle over a boat dock on their Minnesota property, and therefore could not complete their sale there. They were in a quandary what to do. So we offered to take over their payments here, purchasing their property from them. While it was not the house we wished to retain, it helped us out as well as them. In turn, our daughter and husband had sold their little house near Aurora just before the new baby was born, and needed a place to live while they were having their new home built. So we moved our belongings into the garage there, and allowed them to live in the house. We lived in our motor home on the acreage, some of the time, but mostly travelled into Minnesota overseeing our lands there. So the little house that we really did not want to purchase, amply served both families for a while. We sold it later to a couple who improved it and lived there many years.

We continued to find what we considered bargains in land from time to time, investing without the day to day duties of running the office. It was a welcome respite. This gave us more time to travel if we desired, often to Minnesota. That country seemed to be a sleeping giant as far as land prices were concerned. But there were those cold winters to contend with. There were many folks with Norwegian or Swedish background. We found many dear friends among these hard working folks. We were amused one day when a little old lady said she could tell we were "from the south", not realizing we had any accent; when all the while we could not understand her Swedish brogue at all. There seemed to be a certain amount of friction between the Norwegians and the Swedes, each especially desiring their own customs and special foods. One day I heard a Swedish lady declaring very strongly she hoped she did not have a drop of Norwegian blood in her, but, if she found she did, she would take pills for it. Most had great senses of humor.

We grew to love the people, especially many close friends in the Baptist Church in Fosston, Minnesota. The Pastor and his wife, the Winchesters, came to visit us in MO. one time. Another couple, the Andersons, visited us more than once. They since have become part-time farmer missionaries to the Ukraine. Another couple, the Hanson's, sold us part of their land when they were down-sizing. They also were very craft-oriented, and we purchased for our living room a large wooden clock he had made. During the short time, we lived in a house we purchased in Fosston, we enjoyed going out to their barn where they sold crafts. This was originally an old tall hay barn, in excellent condition. They hired experts who professionally cut down the entire barn lowering it under the same roof, so that it was a beautiful modern looking structure. They had documented the several days of the entire procedure on camcorder. So interesting. It still housed a loft-like area dubbed "The Upper Room" used by the youth group from the church.

Itchy Feet

I don't think foot powder solves this condition. Keith was feeling the need to be busier, wanting to get back to Missouri and suggesting we look into starting up a United Farm Real Estate Office again. So we made the move to Clinton, MO., where a man-made lake area was filling with water, inviting new residents. While there were realtors in the area, none representing United Farm, so this looked ideal for United as well as us. As time went on, every possible location we attempted to obtain that would be suitable for an office, seemed to be exorbitant in price or with unreasonable restrictions. The National Agency tried to help us, but it didn't work out.

Then the Agency questioned us as to feasibility for us to move on further south to Marshfield. The Agent there had died suddenly and they had been limping along without a broker agent. An office was already active in Young's Shopping Center just off the Interstate Highway. We looked it over and also found a white brick house across the Interstate from the Office that was for sale. So we made the purchase and the move. It was good to be nearer family again than when in northern Minnesota. I was happy about that, too. We had a large territory and found it to be satisfactory for us, as we both worked hard at it.

My Mother had been a widow for a couple years by this time and considered coming from Iowa to Marshfield by bus to visit us. Pretty courageous on her part, as most of her life had been centered around her home and farming. We found that while the bus had no regular bus station in our town, it did make a stop at the Interstate off ramp intersection for anyone getting on or off. That spot was not far from either our house, or the office, so arrangements were made. We were awaiting her arrival just as instructed, but couldn't believe our eyes—the bus went right on with my Mother in tow. She told the driver she had seen us standing there. When the driver admitted his mistake, his bus was in the middle of the bridge over the Interstate, with cars coming and going. He stopped the bus, opened the door, and let her out. There was not even a shoulder of safety for her to stand on until we could literally run up to where she was and rescue her. We got her safely off the bridge. Then spoke sternly to the bus authorities about such a delivery of an aging nearly blind passenger. They could not have been more unconcerned stating this sort of thing happens when there is not a regular station. So that was our fault?? Truly unbelievable.

We enjoyed the white brick home in Marshfield that had been so well taken care of. However, when a potential veterinary came to our office wanting a good location to set up an office, we could not find what he needed. Our house was an ideal location. However, he really wanted more acres with it. But he made us an offer that worked for him and we sold him our home. He was able to adapt it as he needed and had a successful business for several years. There was a house not far away available for us to rent, so we continued the real estate business for a time.

Keith seemed often to keep his ear to the ground, so to speak, for a good buy in real estate. A few years later, he was told of some land in Ontario, Canada, owned and for sale by an American. The question: was he interested? He wanted more information, so met with the son of the owner in a Greenfield, MO. restaurant, and came home to tell me. It was a 40 acre piece near Larder Lake for $2600. He was given verification of it to show me including snapshots. Apparently this lady owner had owned it a long time, now aged and ill, and wanting to get her affairs in order. Keith and I were never ones to visit casinos or enter into other forms of gambling. We felt whatever possessions we had were from the Lord and we were to be good stewards of them. We had purchased land sight unseen before, but always from a trusted person who represented it. This man and his mother were not known by us, the land was in a foreign country, so to purchase it was taking a risk. We made phone calls to authorities in Canada to verify the truth of it, and decided to purchase it. We considered if we lost the investment, it could be chalked up to our education; perhaps Foreign Land Investment-101.

Well, it was an education. But not until time to sell it. First, when we did make a trip there, it did look as the snapshots pictured it—pretty rugged with large boulders exposed. That was due to long ago attempts to mine gold from the now expired gold claim on it. In 1990, a Quebec resident phoned us with an offer to purchase the acreage for $6,000, which we agreed to. The sale had to be handled by the Canadian government authorities, who collected the money from the buyer. So far, so good. However, the part of our education course that we had not studied for was that since we were foreign owners, we were treated differently than if we lived in Canada. Red flag! The $6000 was held by the government until they determined our (huge) profit on the sale, and then claimed half of it to pay our income tax there. This took them several months, but the day arrived when we received what they felt we should have. We only took that Course one time, since we felt we learned quite a lot first time.

Through the years, we had relocated our residence from Verona farm to Aurora, Marionville, Fosston, MN, Clinton, MO. and then Marshfield, but all the while doing business with our very helpful banker in Monett, MO. One of the officers there was planning to relocate, and wanting to sell his house and part of his acreage north of Monett, and wondered if we might be interested in buying it. We were.

Monett, Missouri

So the next fifteen plus enjoyable years of our lives were at this location. It started in the fall with the purchase of a home and 20 acres on what is now known as Chapel Drive. The name denotes the two country churches located on this highway. Our home was between the two. From the start our plan was to live in the existing home while building a new home north of it. Then resell the original home with 3 acres, leaving 17 acres on which to build our new home. We began collecting information on various brands of pre-manufactured homes, and settled on a Wick Home due to the good quality of materials and workmanship they use. The whole project was a very interesting experience. The contractual agreement specifies everything that makes up the entire house, which is virtually pre-built in Wisconsin. When it arrived by way of several semi trucks, it consisted of some walls totally built, others in sections to be put together later. The two bathrooms were completely built with plumbing and doors to be added later. The engineering of the ordering, filling of the order, putting it together when it arrived, etc. was a major task. There were definitely some glitches along the way, which would be true of any method of building. Most workers on site were excellent, and some not so much. For instance, a worker who proclaimed loudly how he had never had a leak in his work sweating copper plumbing, did not measure up to that on this job. Here when the water was turned on, it could have irrigated a garden if our basement had been hovering over it. He was one who often needed to run into town for "supplies" on company time, but we learned that the supplies were all liquid in a bottle and seemed to affect his ability to function. His "work" ended abruptly. Another time after the building was nearly completed, even draperies and sheers hung, but no carpeting, a buckle developed in living room floor. A conscientious worker came to fix it and then sand it off smooth. Not wanting to catch the curtain sheers in the sander he made a poor decision by tying a knot it them. It did keep them out of the way. The Company had to pay to have them removed, pressed and re-hung. Wick Homes did do everything their contract stated. The end result was, we were pleased with the Wick house.

Many extras were added by us, including a wood burning furnace in the basement ducted through the house. This was very satisfactory, and we attached it to the water heater, so that it also preheated the water. Because of the furnace, other people became interested in a similar arrangement. This opened the way for us to become salesmen for the furnaces in the area. Earlier we also had a wood burning fireplace built, which was not used as much as we had thought, due to the efficiency of the furnace. Another extra was a wrap-around deck at the back and side of the house. Many a barbecue, games with the grandkids, visiting times, or watching a beautiful sunrise was really enjoyed.

Monett home

One of Keith's dreams was realized. It included a large metal shed with room to house the motor home, tractor, trailer and a workshop in one end. He also had a pond built and stocked it with catfish. The fish grew accustomed to a person coming to the edge of the pond—food in hand. It was fun to watch them jostle for extra gulps, and they did grow. However, we noticed a lowering of the water, so knew that the usual was happening—a slow leak due to rocky soil. We tried various remedies, but all to no avail, and the fish raising enterprise had to be stopped.

When we purchased the land, the previous owners had planted many shade and evergreen trees making a nursery. The intention had been to sell them when smaller, but that didn't happen. By the time we purchased the land the trees had already suffered from overcrowding. We were able to sell some of the trees to nurseries active in business. A tree digging machine was used for some, but roots were so intertwined and deep, not always successful. Some were dug and balled by manual labor. When that did work alright, the height and age of the tree made for a premium sale. But that could easily involve a full day's hard work per tree. We left that task to those who had the know-how. We also gave some of smaller, easier to manage trees to our family members. Several of those pines at our daughter's homes grew to lovely, still growing trees. We replanted many on our own acreage, making a grove along our north boundary. When they did have a favorable transplanting experience, they loved the new breathing space and grew quickly. Soon, this grove of pines became a favorite hide-and-seek spot for our preteen grandsons. I think Jesse James or the Dalton Brothers may have entered into their play.

Keith and I have always enjoyed gardening and this acreage offered a good spot near our eastern border, not as rocky as some. Through the years we would raise more tomatoes, green beans, potatoes, asparagus, strawberries, blueberries and even wild blackberries than we could use for ourselves. So we offered produce for sale. I tried various methods of selling, some quite time consuming. So I began using the telephone, stating after they would agree to purchase for a certain price, that when we delivered it, if they were dissatisfied, then there was no sale. That never did occur. I sold to restaurants, nursing homes, schools as well as individuals. That perhaps would not be allowed now if food now requires inspection. But then, that was never an issue. So far as I know, there were no casualties!

Keith and I had a gardening routine. We would declare war on the weeds one day and then to "rest" would load up our produce and deliver it the next day. I delivered some to the senior citizens' apartments, but I didn't continue. This was time consuming, as each lonely senior citizen would insist on our coming in to visit. I understood their need, but time was of the essence before the end of the day when delivery was promised. A lot of the staff members in our bank were good and appreciative customers. We enjoyed doing this, and were often the only source for fresh produce available.

Once Keith's Mother from Iowa, who was widowed by then, had come to visit us for a week, and stayed for six or seven weeks. I told her she was "The Lady Who Came to Dinner". Actually the choice was not hers. She had been having angina pains previously, but this bout resulted in her having open heart surgery to correct the problem. She was 87 years old. That is not an unusual age for such a procedure these days, but it was then. So much so that the newspaper came and featured a story about her being the oldest person ever to have that type surgery at that hospital. So she not only competed in the literary world with "The Man Who Came to Dinner", she broke into the media world as well. I think she would have willingly traded it all for an easier solution.

Another memorable time also involved a visit from relatives. Dick and Roberta, my cousin and her husband, were leaving their home in Peoria, IL. in winter seeking warmer weather and pulling a camper trailer. They decided on a stop-over at our Monett, Missouri home before going further south. We so looked forward to their coming. However, temperature was at the freezing mark and a misty rain had fallen all day, coating trees, fences, electric lines, and vehicles, but, fortunately the highways were too warm to be frozen. So they arrived, as planned, and we had a great reunion. As the afternoon wore on, tree limbs were becoming heavy, a few were breaking off. Utility lines were stretching to the ground, pulling some poles over with them, blocking some roads. Our electric power was off. My cooking range was propane gas, so we could have cooked meals: supper by candle light and kerosene lamp. We played a board game by the same lighting—lots of laughs. But the freezing misty rain did not stop. Dick made sure their furnace ran OK in their camper, so off to their bed they went. Of course, our heat was from wood source, so our house was warm, and we urged the visitors to sleep in our spare bedroom. But they preferred their regular sleeping quarters—for the first part of the night, that is. It is hard to describe the eerie feeling that comes in complete, total darkness. Add to that the intermittent sounds of tree limbs breaking off high up in a tree, then come clattering down to the ground through ice-laden limbs. Dick and Roberta moved themselves into the house for the remainder of the night. However, that location was not a lot better, as large windows beside the bed didn't make for much relaxation for sleep. It could be that a tree limb might crash through the window and the deep darkness did not reveal from whence the sounds came. It was a long night. The next day was a repeat. Our yard full of nearly 100 year old oak trees were casting off many of their limbs, even clogging our driveway. The pine grove I mentioned earlier was toppling its trees over, roots and all from the previous abundant rain plus the excessive weight of the ice buildup.

Our neighbor who joined us on the south was glad to see his daughter drive in safely from her home in southern IL. He chose a spot for her to park her brand new car where limbs would not be falling. The next morning it was a shock to see a tree farther away had uprooted and was tall enough to fall across her car. Not a preferred maiden voyage for a new car. Also not a thing you are anxious to tell your insurance agent about, either.

Our visitor, Dick, an excellent electrician, was able to wire our motor home generator up to our power source, so that we could have minimum power to run our refrigerator and freezer. A real blessing since the actual electric company did not turn our power back on for several days. Their job over the whole territory was beyond my comprehension. Electric Companies from several states sent linemen to assist. We could all see that this situation was becoming a marathon, rather than a sprint. Dick and Roberta began to check to see what direction they would need to go to get out of the "ice age" the quickest, as they felt they needed to move on. We also were clearing our driveway best we could to make it passable. Keith hoped his plan for the toppled pines would save at least some of them by using the tractor loader to lift them back up into their original root socket hole, and then use ropes to secure them until they could reestablish their root contact and grow again. It did work for some of them. Others were too broken.

We hated to see Dick and Roberta leave, but they ventured out and phoned us later that they had made their escape from ice prison safely. She later wrote that their "short stop over" to our home was the highlight of their trip for the winter. We had also been trying to leave for the south, but had to get some order in our devastated front yard before leaving. The task was monumental. Our two grandsons, (you know the Dalton Brothers) came and helped us so much. We have had other ice storms since, but this Granddaddy of them all will not be forgotten.

It was enjoyable to be able to travel during some of the winters, in south Texas, New Mexico or in Arizona. One trip was to Florida. My sister, Dorothy and her husband also had a motor home and several times they came from Iowa to Missouri and we traveled together. We made several trips to northern Minnesota where we purchased land from time to time. One trip in the summer, my cousin Roberta and her husband in their car and trailer traveled with us into Minnesota. We were grateful for the many travel experiences we were able to enjoy while health permitted.

After we had spent a few winters in campgrounds in and around Mission, Texas, we learned of a place called Bibleville, near Alamo. It is a 40 acre conference grounds, and is for people who know Christ as Savior including from all church denominations. It offers various ways to volunteer, for instance, to help build a church, work at an orphanage in Mexico, sewing comforts or clothing, making Vacation Bible School material, to name a few. During each of these that I participated in, the work was accomplished amidst laughter, good times and sweet fellowship. There were also many opportunities to play. The 215 campsites, as well as permanent homes on the grounds, housed retired missionaries, pastors and laymen in general. Try to imagine the difference between this place and the atmosphere in the average campground. Of all the days we spent during our years at Bibleville, I never even one time heard foul language, filthy stories, saw anyone smoking or drinking alcohol, to mention a few differences. Talent seemed to be unending, with outstanding performances given in the 800 plus seat comfortable auditorium. Well known Bible teachers were guests to hold week long conferences. Visitors from the area campgrounds came often to enjoy the music, plays, and conferences. We wished we had learned of this delightful place earlier, but were able to spend four winters there before Keith's health problems became an issue

Bibleville in Texas

Spending winters at Bibleville, we still lived in Monett, Mo and had found an excellent church—First Baptist there. Several young couples attended and I was so privileged to be their Sunday-School teacher. We outgrew the classroom, and fixed up an unused small room, that by removing a false wall hiding a previously forgotten area became ample for our need. Those couples, and some singles, were no doubt more of a help to me, than I was to them.

I cannot leave the subject of our Monett home without mentioning monumental changes in the property several years after it was under new ownership. Changes occurred May 4, 2003 when a monstrous tornado roared through the countryside, wiping out part of Pierce City, then continuing on north of Monett, devastating a mobile home park west of the Monett house. It continued on. The lovely aged oaks in the front yard that had withstood many a previous storm were no match for this one. Virtually all the pine grove was wiped out. The northwest corner of the house was hit, damaging the roof and some of the deck. The large shed/shop looked like it escaped damage—until you went inside. The vacuum had been so intense it caved in most of the east wall of the building.

Though we lived some miles away, our learning of the storm across what had been such familiar territory to us just had to be investigated. It was hard to keep our bearings when landscapes had been removed. We didn't recognize our former property at first, and then caught a glimpse of the house still standing back behind the huge oak trees, twisted and on the ground. Keith was able to pull off the road into the edge of the drive. We had to sit there a while to grasp what had happened. Amidst the chaos was a striking view of a neat stack of 4 foot lengths of the big logs. We knew the present owner was partially disabled, so wondered how the logs could have been sawed. We observed him coming out of the house, walking with two canes. Keith went to greet him. They fell into each other's arms and cried. He told us he was in the basement during the storm and was safe. His wife was in another town working. Then he said that very soon after the winds, a group of Amish folks whom he had never met, came and began cleaning up some of the debris. They included men, women and even children. They brought chain saws and salvaged what they could of the valuable logs. The homeowner told them to arrange to come back and get the logs to sell them to repay them for their work. But they declined stating that he no doubt needed whatever income he could get for them. This type of kind act is repeated over and over by Amish people following a storm.

Ten years prior to the storm, is when we had sold the Monett house. Since we needed a new home, we saw a "reduced price ad" for a house in Republic, so went to investigate. It was a lovely brick home that truly needed some TLC. We could see that structurally it was worthy of fixing, so purchased it and moved there. Up till then, I didn't think it was possible to ever have too many built-in cabinets and storage, but this house proved that to be false—certainly more than I could fill. And they were so beautifully done. So that part needed no attention. The property included an extra fenced-in lot, so was a good place to park the motor home. We had looked forward to being closer to Springfield, so purchased the home, but the location was noisy and heavily travelled. After looking it over, our son-in-law predicted we would live there a year. Hmmm. Pretty close, it was a year and a week. But our hard work paid off as we resold it to parents of a local businessman.

Adventures Continue

For some time, we considered building a house/shop—sort of hybrid. In our travels we saw a few of these and could see how it would fit our need. It may be better described as a large shop/storage shed with an attached home. While we lived in the Republic house, I took measurements of the parts of the house we liked the best, and drew a blueprint, of sorts, so it would house our motor home. The storage shed part would have access to heat and A/C, running water and sewer access; therefore it would furnish living quarters year round in the RV, thus making a smaller two bedroom home adequate. We could envision how adaptable for us this would be, and cost effective at the same time.

When we saw an ad for a 160 acre property that included a house site (previously for a mobile home) all located in northern Lawrence County, we got enthused. So checked it out, loving the small stream that flowed close to where the mobile home had been, as well as a constant flowing spring spouting out of the ground. Keith could immediately see how perfect the woods were for hunting, as well. We even saw where useable flat sandstones were formed. Of course, we did not need such a large acreage, but anticipated selling off part for a building site or two, thus recouping part of the investment. So we purchased it, parking our motor home on the house site.

To move us to this new location, we had purchased an enclosed large delivery truck and carefully packed our belongings into it to store. We sorted them so access to what would be needed for this "gypsy" move would be at the back of the truck. A "modern" convenience was our automatic washing machine. You simply go up a plank to the back of the truck, lift the overhead door, plug the machine into electric power, fill the machine with cold water from the hydrant-hooked water hose, add cold water soap, arrange the drain hose so it flowed on the ground outside the truck add clothes and let it do its thing. It worked great!

The clothes dryer was an older type model known as fresh air, a clothesline and two well placed trees. There were no other houses even close, so we were private in our wash day woods-hideaway. Try to imagine one such wash day—me dressed in my end of the available clothes garb, when in drives a vehicle for a visit. Out steps a man and woman, one looks familiar—our grandson. He had come to introduce his very special lady friend for the first time. Can you comprehend what kind of impression she had of this whole scene? And the disappointment our grandson must have had who had driven from another state to show her his grandparents! Like I said, she was a special lady. She still chose to become part of our family. There have been times in later years, when she, with a twinkle in her eye, refers to those relatives who are trailer trash. Very recently, they have built a new home in a woodsy setting, and I notice they have a semi-trailer truck bed toward the back of their property, being used for storage. No comment.

We so enjoyed many things about this acreage. But it seemed, any way we mentally attempted to divide it, was not feasible. There was no way we could handle all the 160 acres. We also could not live in our motor home during the winter in that climate, and winter was ever drawing closer. As much as we hated to, we would have to give up our plan to build our dream hybrid home. We had an inquiry of someone who was interested in purchasing the land, strictly for hunting. We got together with him and made the sale.

Home by Stockton Lake

It was then that we purchased a home and 4 acres near Stockton Lake. The Lake was not visible, but was a short walk to its edge. When this Lake was built the Corp of Engineers purchased all water front lands. We not only could walk, but could drive our tractor, pulling our fishing boat down the trail to the water's edge, thereby launching our boat. It was during this time that I truly began to enjoy fishing. The convenience of it was wonderful. Sometimes, we would go fishing just after dawn, and by the time the fish quit biting, could head for shore, and then to the house. Or we could go at dusk. Even if a rain cloud appeared, it was a short jaunt back to the house.

Others all along the Lake area enjoyed similar privileges. No doubt, you have heard the expression "You are just having too much fun." This must have been the reasoning behind the official closings of some of these spots. We began to get word of this, so checked it out for ourselves. Some were actual old roads that had tons of gravel rocks dumped on them to prevent access. When land owners would prove to the Corp that these were public roads that were used before the Lake covered them with water, and that they could not be closed, then they had to move the tons of rock. Other accesses remained closed. Those of us in our subdivision wondered if we might be next, but we wondered very quietly.

One day the new Conservation Agent came to our house, guess we were the ones who were home. Anyway, he told us that in about a year, our access to the water would be closed. They would do it immediately, but didn't have the funds. It seems that the Corp of Engineers (federal) had leased all the shoreline land to the Missouri Conservation (state) to manage it, seed it, etc. Lease cost was $1.00 per year!

We asked why it was to be closed. He said we were trampling endangered species of flowers, as well as hurting the rocks! After his visit, he went back to his office in town. We contacted other landowners in our subdivision, and some of us agreed to meet with him at his office the next morning. We presented our case to him that we kept the trail and launching area mowed. Also since the launching area is often used by other boaters for a party area, we kept trash, beer bottles, and such all picked up and disposed of. It seemed the Agent had his hearing aid turned off. We asked him if he would meet with us and show us the flowers we were endangering. He did come, but couldn't find any endangered flowers. Guess our damage was complete. He also had said we made big ruts as we launched. He couldn't find this, either.

Remember what he told us—it would be closed in a year because they needed funds for cable and posts, etc. The next morning, a metal gate across entrance, was double chained and padlocked to a steel post set part way across the entrance. Perhaps their ship had come in to that small launching area? The smaller entrance was still wide enough for their big brush hogs to come through to mow. They still burned off huge areas for controlled burns. Poor, poor endangered flowers.

After our objecting to the Conservation Agent, his answer was simple. He could not make any other decision since his orders came from the Corps of Engineers. We decided, since the land was really owned by the Corps, to go see them at their location by the Lake. This took a while since many other irate fishermen and land owners whose access had been blocked were present, almost had to pick a number. But our turn came. We stated our concern. The pat answer, that could have been a recording, was that they, the federal government, relinquished all their authority, when they leased the lakeshore land to the State of Missouri Conservation. Quite a bit of authority for $1.00 per year. But I should ask you: Did you enjoy this merry-go-round ride with us? According to others who had been on it much longer than we, since the circle goes nowhere, we might as well get off. This was a disappointment, to say the least. We were never given a valid reason. Now we would have to license our boat for road travel, drive quite a distance to wait our turn to launch in a very popular public area, after buying a permit that you put in a box on an honesty basis. It is more hassle and inconvenience to boat owner, than real income to the Corp.

One thing we both enjoyed about the location of our home was the abundant wildlife we would see often; particularly deer. On a moonlit night, there were times we could see them outside our bedroom window grazing. Or in daylight hours, there were fawns curled up under a big shade tree nearby. If that happened, there would usually be a hoof stomping mamma close by to get their attention and alert them to the dangerous people that lived there.

Deer in front yard

We were not fond of the armadillos who took over our lawn, digging up rocks as they went, as if they owned the place and paid the taxes. If lawnmowers could tote a picket sign, it would state "Down with armadillos who ruin lawnmower blades."

I realize black snakes are harmless to humans, and help them by catching mice and other varmints. If only they could read and learn where their territory is and is not. For instance, when we noticed several items on the floor in the garage below a high storage shelf, we wondered how that happened. Later, we saw a blacksnake edging his way up the wall. Apparently, mamma snake, already up on the shelf, must have called daddy snake to supper. Or something. They often are in pairs. So Keith was able to get them both in tow and take them on the scenic route deeper into the woods to continue their life together. It wasn't till some time later, when Keith and I were both mowing grass on our four acres surrounding our house that I spotted a slithering "friend". I ran for a hoe, and was able to pin him down. I kept calling for Keith to stop his mower and help, but he was unable to hear over the roar of the mowers. Finally, he did see me and came. A quick silent vote was taken by he and I designating the days of scenic routes over, and time for taps.

Now copperheads, a completely different topic due to their poisonous venom, which starts at birth. Interestingly, the birth is a live birth. Our paths almost never crossed, however. We used a shortcut through the woods to the road beyond. Keith always carried a heavy walking stick when he went across. Good thing he did this one day. Not one, but two copperheads declared the path to be their own. Keith won the argument. He hung them over his stick to transport them to the hard surface of the gravel road, stretching them out to measure. My memory fails me now as to their length, but I do remember that it was longer than the Conservation publication stated was the maximum. We had already learned not to consider everything they said. The yardstick, not ink, was the proof.

Another form of wildlife in this beautiful spot was wild flowers the lady owner that preceded me had planted. Some I knew the names of and some I did not. Approximate size of this flower bed was 90 to 100 feet long by about 3 feet across that paralleled the road. Passersby would stop to enjoy. While I enjoyed it from my living room picture window, if it really flourished as it should, there was not time to stop to enjoy. Not when the grass mowing was nearly constant, a large garden needing weeding, hoeing, harvesting, and, of course, a few pool games. Also Rummikub between Keith and I needed tending. I love beautiful flowers, but I determined it doesn't take that many to be beautiful—ever again.

During the 10 years we lived there, other wild things included one lightning strike that creamed our heat pump compressor, two hail storms in consecutive years, severe enough to require a roof shingle replacement each time. But we remained safe, and enjoyed a lot of very good weather and a good garden spot.

We have some photos of huge tomatoes, cantaloupes, and climbing okra that was a blooming beauty all its own. Our garden had chain link fence all around that kept out the deer; well almost until a few learned of treasures inside the fence and would simply glide over the top. Squirrels can't be bothered by an obstacle like small holes in a fence to get through. Somehow they can stretch out enough to slide through. But the journey back through with a tomato, ripe or green, that is larger than the hole, now there is a problem. Also, that line-up of their too large, harvested tomatoes all along the fence left a bit of nasty evidence behind. But we humans were severely outnumbered and had to surrender.

One lasting memory from this Dade County location was the several long time friends, especially at the Greenfield Senior Citizen's Center. While living there, we continued attending New Home Church in northern Lawrence County, however. It was small, but mighty. Since most members were up in years, we were concerned that in a few years, it would die out. Keith used to pray for an attendance of 40. Occasionally, we would hit that. It wasn't until after we sold our Greenfield home and relocated to Aurora to be closer to Springfield medical facilities. After we changed churches, New Home started to grow. We used to tell the pastor that it was necessary first to get rid of the riff-raff. Our close friend from the church would keep us posted from time to time as to the growth. We were so happy for them. Many children and youth began to attend—just what was needed. Baptismal waters were needed often. Eventually the time came after we had moved away that a new addition to the building was added, and then even later, the Pastor was called to be full time Pastor instead of bi-vocational like he had been for so many years. Wonderful blessings for any church, but in this remote location such growth was remarkable.

We lived in the Greenfield location for 10 years. A large portion of that time, there was no medical doctor in the entire county. Thankfully we had not needed one. But during 2003 and 2004, Keith had needed hip replacement surgery and extensive back surgery. The tests, surgery, and therapy needed called for many trips into the south end of Springfield, which was a round trip total of approximately 70 miles. We began to consider a move closer to medical facilities. (Of great importance also was the fact there was not a Wal-Mart in our whole county. Just how does one function without a Wal-Mart store? ☺

Seriously, a couple did come to purchase our home on 4 acres. They liked it due to the close proximity to Stockton Lake and also they had former neighbors in another city, who would again be their neighbors in the new location. So we began a search for the ideal place for what would become our 20th move, contemplating it to be our last one. We were grateful for each move that had contributed to our income through the years as we fixed each one up for resale. After we chose a brick home in Aurora, it provided for a more manageable size to take care of. Keith would describe its qualities to friends by saying "It is a block to the Senior Center, a couple blocks to the hospital, and a few blocks to the nursing home." One response that made him laugh was "And how far to the cemetery?" I guess that did fit the whole aging scenario. And sure enough that did eventually find its way into our picture, though a different cemetery.

Aurora, Missouri

Since we had lived in this town during our active real estate days, in many ways the town was familiar. But in many ways it had changed. The First Baptist Church in Aurora was going through a difficult time, so we decided to visit First Baptist Church in Marionville. We fell in love with the people and the Pastor and the message proclaimed there, so made it our home church. That was the right thing to do, continuing on for several years. Not only did we profit greatly from the Bible preaching, Keith was able to express his love of music with solos from time to time. I eventually became a part time teacher of an adult Sunday School Class. The two of us together shared in chapel services at a nursing home in Monett and another one in Marionville. His part involved singing, and mine was to write short devotionals to share with the group. These times were special, at least to us. We also began volunteering at the Senior Citizen's Center, taking care of flowers and shrubbery for five years. For a short period, we delivered meals to shut-ins. Later I was elected to serve on the Board of Directors, an interesting experience.

These enjoyable years included continuing to travel in our motor home including one more winter in Bibleville in south

Texas. Keith continued to be a good driver for this "travel train". But preparation became more difficult for him to do all that is necessary to prepare the rig and the tow car, as well as packing for the prolonged stay for winter. His right hip that was replaced by surgery earlier was never satisfactory, resulting with weakness, lameness, and a feeling that the new hip socket was not tight. So after four years, we investigated a different surgeon for a hip revision. This involved removal of the previous prosthesis (no small task) and replace it with one that fit. The original cap was found to be too large for the ball, so no wonder it threatened to pop out with every step. Recovery from this surgery took a long time, and still resulted in his need for a cane. While it was not ever like the one given him at birth, it was better than the first replacement.

Our motor home travels allowed various types of visits offering all the comforts of home. It was a combination taxi/motel/restaurant—sort of a turtle-travel—carrying our house on our back. But we had to acknowledge a need for change. The Book of Proverbs admonishes us "There is a time for everything". For some reason, there is no mention of a need to sell a motor home, but we still applied the truth to our situation and sold our comfortable vehicle. It has been a joy to hear from the new owners of their enjoyment of it, as well.

Our preference had always been to live in the country, but we adjusted to living in town. We each had slowed our pace so took advantage of life in this small town.

Three annual occasions in this town stand out in my memory. One is the local Business Fair. Merchants set up their booths that publicize their service or merchandise, and offer door prizes each 30 minutes announced by the local Radio Station, who also has a booth. They make a celebration of it all, and we often see many friends there as well.

The second is Senior Appreciation Day put on by the Aurora School System. They set up tables in the gymnasium to seat hundreds within the district for a lovely free meal, prepared by the school, served efficiently in a matter of minutes by the teachers and students. A program that features school pupils in various displays of their talents, also recognizing the oldest person attending, those in the military, and those who have paid the supreme price. It is so well planned, and each year we come away with a feeling of pride in our school and today's youth. The reason given for this annual occurrence is so the school can show appreciation to the elderly who continue to pay school taxes, though they no longer have children in school. I have not heard of another School District that does this. It gives us pride and appreciation for all of them, as well.

The third is an annual Thanksgiving Day meal offered by the First Methodist Church in town to anyone who comes, particularly emphasizing those who might otherwise be alone. It always is an abundant cafeteria style meal with a chance to donate to it, if you wish. I am impressed by the large number of their church who forfeit their own family Thanksgiving Day, as well as prior to the Day, to offer this service. Following the meal, there is a chance to choose from the large tables displayed on the stage that feature pies and other desserts. Since it was difficult for Keith to maneuver the steps up to view this display, I offered to go and return with the report, then I could go back to make the choice. For some reason, the large tables on the stage had come out closer than usual to the edge, plus the fact I was not paying close attention, as I stepped backward off the stage, tumbling "gracefully?" down the steps. This in front of all the many people enjoying their meal. Quite a scene I created. Boy Scouts and others rushed to my rescue wanting to help me up. I thought I could get up by myself if I could take a moment to clear out the stars that appeared with the crash. And so I did, being more embarrassed than injured. At least, that is what I thought. So I walked back to my table, and others delivered our pie.

Our car was already packed to drive on to Arkansas to visit our daughter and husband for a family reunion of a few days. Keith thought we should go back home, but I thought all was well, so we went on. As time went on, I had to rely more and more on Keith's extra cane he had in the car. It soon became my constant companion, as I learned later on that I had cracked my pelvis. There is no procedure to fix that anyway, except for 6 to 8 weeks of healing time.

Nearing the end of our journey

The Unwelcome Diagnosis

Keith was already scheduled to see a gastroenterologist to determine why he had some discomfort in his stomach, as well as some weight loss. So we kept the appointment that included, among other tests, an endoscopy to view the inside of his stomach. The doctor spoke to me afterward that he saw a very small growth that he considered insignificant, but did take a sample to send away for further testing. Several days later in the evening, beyond regular office hours, the doctor phoned our home. His reluctant voice seemed to be searching for just the right words to give us the news that admittedly astonished him, and certainly did us. This "insignificant growth biopsy" revealed that Keith had non-Hodgkins lymphoma. He asked Keith if he had a preference of an oncologist. Keith's stunned reply was that he had not been looking for one. So, the doctor said he would choose one for him, and chose Dr. Ruth Grant. What we didn't know then, but definitely learned later, that we were given what we considered to be, the cream of the crop at Hulston Cancer Center. They soon phoned us later to start the first of many appointments there.

We asked our daughter and son in law to go with us to our first visit with Dr. Grant. A lot of walking was expected, and sometimes rapid to follow medical staff. Keith was consistently slow as he used a cane, and due to what our son in law now dubbed as my "pie dive", I was also slow and needing a cane. So this was the start of our dual wheelchair parade powered by our kids, down many a hall or into an elevator, or office space. We were grateful for this help, repeated many times over.

Following our introduction to Dr. Grant, her first sentence to Keith was "You have a very dangerous, fast growing, malignant cancer, not curable, but treatable; however your age is against you, but your good health with no smoking or drinking favors you." Now that was a sentence that takes time to digest! Keith asked her what his choices were, recalling horror stories we had heard from some who had taken chemo treatments. She speaks with such clarity, yet with great caring in her voice. Her concise answer: "You have two choices—chemo treatments, or hospice."

Keith's lymph nodes immediately were swelling to such an extent that a few days later he was hospitalized thus accelerating his scans, and other tests, and chemo treatments were started. We were off and running on a rapid roller coaster ride of less than 8 months. He had no horror stories to add regarding his chemo treatments, as each time, they were so diligently given with much intravenous medicine that prevented any vomiting. The most difficult part for him was several incidents a vein would refuse this strong medicine, and he would have more needle sticks. Usually a port is surgically installed, but his treatments were started quickly during his hospital stay, and the port had not been installed.

Our many visits to Hulston Cancer Center resulted in seeing some of the same people each time, and enjoyed some good friendships. The staff there could not have been more helpful or caring, making sure the patient and the accompanying helper were comfortable. For instance a cabinet full of blankets or a knitted throw were available, soft drinks, as well. Workers always seemed to be cheery and in good spirits. Coming each day to face a room full of sick people, and in some instances—very sick, could surely be a downer. Some also had baby-sitting or other problems at home. Yet the priority was the patient. Volunteers contributed much toward the patient. For instance, trained dogs were sometimes brought on a leash for the patient to pet and talk to if he wished. My favorite volunteer was a lady who brought a very small harp. She would sit to one side, and play soothing, calming music. Speaking of music, the Center arranges for volunteers to play the piano on the first floor, as you enter. A patient may enter with fear or dread, but those familiar, beautiful hymns soon changed that focus. I made it a point to always go to the pianist to thank him or her. What a blessing their volunteering was!

Keith's body responded well to the chemo treatments. This, too, was a blessing, as he often throughout his life, reacted to medicines. I know some patients still get very ill during treatment, and he just did not. He mentioned that he reaped the benefit of years of learning about lymphomas, and other cancers, with improved methods of treating it. It was 13 years previously that my brother's wife died of non-Hodgkins lymphoma, and 9 years since my sister died of the same disease. Some ways to treat it had been improved. So that wonderful summer day, the repeated tests for Keith revealed that his cancer was in remission. That was a day of rejoicing on our part!

I had been battling a bad cold (in summer!) and it had settled in my bronchial tubes, and then went further. Perhaps I felt it was my turn to be ill, so had to enter the hospital with pneumonia. It was not many days later, when Keith began experiencing headaches, even waking in the night with pain. It was unusual for him to have headaches. He began to lose his appetite. This was perplexing, to say the least, for a patient whose cancer was in remission. He clung tenaciously to that remission status, praising the Lord with gratefulness at every opportunity. Finally, as he was again vomiting, I made the decision to take him to Cox Hospital ER, to get some help. They soon admitted him, and started tests, including a CT of his brain. This showed five tumors on his brain. His previous scans always included "from the eyes to the thighs". The brain was not included. As that dear lady, Dr. Ruth Grant, later made a special trip to his room stating her apology for not having included a scan of his brain; I was stunned to hear her apology. I answered her that she owed us nothing. She had worked tirelessly through the months answering phone calls, and numerous questions, sometimes at odd hours, always trying to be of help, but always in control. We both were so grateful for her wisdom and expertise.

When I arrived at Keith's room the next morning, after the scans and his being admitted, he smiled in recognition, but did not speak. I asked if he had breakfast, and he didn't seem to know.

So I inquired, and then ordered his breakfast. When it arrived, he started to eat, but was very deliberate, tarrying with each bite. Certainly this was not his usual self of activity. I continued to talk to him, but no words from him. Then I noticed him struggle to attempt to speak, so I came close. With some effort he began to "want to tell you something". Forming a word at a time into a sentence, his message was, "You and I are in the arms of Jesus forever." That sentence, formed with great difficulty, stating a profound truth, was and still is, a real treasure to me.

It must have been middle to late morning after his breakfast tray was gone, that his legs and arms suddenly began to convulse violently. I tried to hold him to keep him from falling from the bed. I had never seen anyone having a seizure, but thought this may be one, as I frantically phoned the nurses' station. They came running from all directions. I stayed out of their way and wondered what was happening to him. Tears rolled down my cheeks. After a while, they made him stable, but nearly immediately, a second seizure just as violent, followed the first one. This caused a frantic urgency as to his condition, and arrangements were made to transfer him to the Nueeurotrauma Unit. A semblance of order began to emerge from the chaos as the rapid transfer was made down the hall and into the service elevator. NTU was ready for him as well as doctors and other experts, reviewing his case.

There were decisions to be made as to what extent life support was to be given. Keith and I had agreed that we did not want a prolonged life support that only kept the body breathing mechanically, yet we wanted life giving measures if other conditions warranted this. How do you put all this in writing for the healthcare staff before you know the details? His critical condition meant there were questions to be answered, papers to sign. I was feeling overwhelmed and very alone, as far as family was concerned. My three children were each travelling in other states. I phoned our oldest granddaughter who works in the same city, just to clue her in on what was happening. She offered to come, and I told her not to, to stay at her job. She stated she was coming. Just as she arrived, a dear friend from church who had been waiting while his wife was having a treatment in a nearby facility, had decided to come visit Keith in his room, having no idea of the recent events. The nurses on that other floor had directed him to the NTU. I cannot adequately express or ever forget the feeling I had as the two came to me at this time. The life and death need was so urgent. My church friend gathered our group of three together calming my spirit by praying to the One who had been in control all along. Great peace settled over me!

One of the doctors and a chaplain came to where I was in the waiting room, and suggested that I needed to give thought as to how very sick Keith was with the five tumors, including a large one above his right eye and a smaller one on the brain stem, and with advanced years, how much did we want to put him through. Then said Keith's body may not be able to handle such trauma. I told him how Keith had been unable to talk coherently all Tuesday morning, then, struggling, said "You and I are in the arms of Jesus forever" and I agreed with him. As I told the doctor this, he smiled and said it sounds like he has taken care of that part. I assured him that was true.

Since our previous written healthcare directive did not make the issue clear, the head of NTU asked to talk with me. I went to their conference room along with our granddaughter, who had also arranged to have her mother, our middle daughter, on speaker phone from Alaska. Keith's condition revealed respiratory failure and renal failure as well as concern that there may be bleeding in the brain. A CT scan proved that negative, thankfully. But he needed help. Would I allow life support to be given? Of course, I would! But my question to the staff was how could I be assured that support would be with-drawn if there was no hope of his getting well? They assured me that we each had the same goal—to give him immediate assistance expecting him to later function on his own. I gave them written permission, and they proceeded with his care. My prayer was that this decision was the right one.

The NTU waiting room is roomy and comfortable enough for those of us needing to stay around the clock. Some pillows and blankets are available on wooden, padded couches long enough to stretch out on. A very busy secretary keeps track of messages, whereabouts of family members, staying in touch with those attending the patient, and on and on. I always let her know if I needed to leave for a few moments. I could go in to visit Keith for short periods of time, but he was unresponsive. I was instructed to talk with him, hold his hand, or whatever might cause a reaction. My grandson had come after his workday, and he did the same for Keith. The staff is so excellent, and they suggested that I would not be in their way if I stayed in the room with him, hoping he might respond to my voice. So they moved in a lounge chair for the night. They attended him constantly. It is virtually a one on one type of care. Sometimes through the night, Keith would move his arms a bit, and the nurse observed his tugging at the life support tube that was down his throat. She prevented him doing that.

About 2 AM, I needed to stretch my legs, so did leave this room for a short walk in the halls. When I returned a staff member came to me in the waiting room to please come back to Keith's area. I feared the worst. Instead, it seemed when no one was looking at him, he had pulled the tube from his throat. This was no small feat, taking a lot of strength. From time to time he became responsive. They wanted me to pull up a regular chair beside his bed and talk to him, stroking his hand, singing, or whatever I thought he might respond to. He tried to speak sometimes, and told me he had gotten rid of that rag they had put down his throat. It made us all smile. I'm sure it was quite uncomfortable. The staff had previously considered removing the tube on a trial basis anyway, since the respirator indicated his breathing was becoming partially his own. He became more and more lucid as time went by, and speaking some, though his throat was sore from the tube. He had questions. Where am I? What happened to me? He still understandably had some confusion, but he wanted to take charge again, a marked improvement. His renal situation continued to be a concern.

Later that day, all doctors agreed that Keith was capable of leaving NTU to go to a room. However, as they removed the brain wave plugs from the top of his head, they observed a sore on his head. A sample was sent to pathology to see if lymphoma cells. No cells were present, but doctor suspects it originated from inside his scalp as lymphoma. The next hurdle we faced was how to choose the best treatment for the tumors of the brain. A doctor in charge of the radiation department was assigned to him. He came several times to visit with Keith. Next day he did talk with Keith about the possibility of radiation, and how it is administered and what result to expect. Keith's advanced age would not prevent the need for aggressive treatment, one each day Monday through Friday for a total of 14. Even with all this, the result is the tumors will only shrink, not be destroyed. A second round of treatments cannot be given. I asked the doctor for statistics of survival if treatment given versus no treatment. His answer, virtually no difference. So now the perplexity of the decision for Keith. These last few days had been weakening, to say the least. Now the weight of such a decision needed, was his. His first thought was to not do them. But the more he thought about it, his desire to fight this enemy that had invaded him, reenergized him. It was that take-charge desire. How would he know if he could win, if he didn't stay in the battle? His decision was a "go", starting in a few days.

Before Keith's dismissal, he was sent to the first floor to do preliminaries for radiation, called a simulation. This is a precise science to fit him with a "bonnet" that marks where each tumor is located. So when he starts treatment, the bonnet directs the radiation to only the exact spot of the tumor, and does not damage good brain cells. Remarkable!

After arriving home from the hospital, Keith was exhausted and resting in bed. Our grandson stopped by on his way home to AR. to let his two kids see Poppy for a few moments. Without any prompting, his not quite 3 year old son, prayed a sweet prayer for his great grand-poppy. This warms the heart of we grandparents to know that our grandchildren are deciding who to turn to in the hour of need!

Keith started his daily, except for weekends, radiation treatments. The treatment itself only took about 15 minutes. But the trip to Springfield and back as he continued to grow weaker, took its toll. Different family members transported us, even as they had been doing for other treatments. I did some of the driving, but not much. I am so grateful for the blessing of family. The help from Hospices had been suggested by one of the radiation doctors. Keith and I decided to pursue it. There are many chapters of Hospice. We asked Dr. Grant her preference, and she said Hospice Compassus and ordered it for us. An admit nurse came to our home and explained it so well to Keith and I. He agreed to sign up; a touching decision for us both. Keith kept going for radiation unless he was too ill to do so.

In the early morning hours of late summer, I knew Keith was restless, but could barely understand his words "I am dying". He repeated it. I did not know if he had had a dream, or if he had come to the realization that his fight was not victorious. I still do not know what was behind it, but I believed his words. Dying was real to him. So I told him I didn't want to tell him good-bye, but I would, and that it was OK for him to go—I would meet him in Heaven. He lay still for a while, and I asked him if he wanted me to read to him from the Bible. He said yes. So I read to him from John 14, verse 1 and on, putting in his name to make it personal. "Keith, don't let your heart be troubled". Jesus telling him "I am going to prepare a home for you, Keith, ... and I will come and take you home to be with me." This seemed to give him contentment.

Less than 3 hours after his "I am dying" statement, he called to me to help him get dressed so he could go to his 9 AM radiation treatment, the 9th in his attempted goal of 14. I could hardly believe it, but called our son-in-law who was willing to take us. It was all Keith could do to go. The doctor well aware of his great weakness, was reluctant to treat him, but did. Keith slept going and coming, and we could hardly get him back in the house and to bed. Hospice nurse made another trip here talking with Keith about radiation. She told him she thought that by now radiation had become a detriment, rather than a help, and he should probably quit the treatments. He had agreed to give radiation a try, and he was certainly not a failure, taking 9 of the 14. The Hospice lady also talked with him about his falling the previous evening, and I had to call for help to get him up. She asked him if he agreed with her that he needed more help to remain safe. Also that it would be more effective for morphine to be given through IV, rather than by liquid like it had been. He agreed with it all, knowing it would mean relocating to a nursing home. I was so grateful he made the decision. I know he would have preferred to remain at home, and so would I. That was part of the reason to go with Hospice. But I was so glad he considered my need for help above his desire to remain at home. That was special.

Our daughter made several inquiries for a place that could take him soon. Due to his condition, some could not, but Aurora Care Center could, and it was just blocks from our home. Getting him there was next. We considered an ambulance, but our daughter and husband thought they could lift him enough into their car to transport him. Then I remembered the OATS bus (Older Adult Transportation System) that has a chair lift mechanism. So phoned for information. Their schedule was full, but that driver offered to come after his full day's work of transporting senior citizens to wherever, and come on his off-duty time. I felt his offer was too much, but he graciously insisted. All I could do was accept and be very grateful. That very afternoon Keith entered ANC by way of the OATS bus, his wheel chair strapped in safely, and accompanied by our kids. Hospice had already delivered a hospital type bed there with side rails and a comfortable air-type mattress, much improved over the nursing home beds.

Keith's care the six days could not have been any more thorough. That included care for me, also, and other family members. A single size bed was in the room, and they made it available for someone to stay around the clock. Some nights two of us stayed, and once both daughters and I stayed. Others had offered to take their turn to stay, but we thought a consistent routine was important. Each meal was delivered to his room, knowing he could not eat, but offering it anyway. So this was sufficient for one of us. Keith did not eat or drink those days, and could not speak. We sang a lot to him, the familiar hymns he loved. Sometimes he moved his lips a bit like he was singing. There were times he would recognize a visitor with a smile, sometimes not.

In recalling those past 8 months, from Keith's diagnosis to what our Pastor describes as "knocking at the door", was a tender growing together of our lives in ways I cannot describe. Some are too private, some defy description. There is something about that word cancer that jolts those who hear it for themselves into an immediate rearrangement of priorities. The quick glimpse into the certainty of eternity changes everything. Several times I was aware of Keith doing things that were a preparation for him to meet his Lord. For instance, when he could still speak, but with effort, he got my attention. I noticed he was close to tears, when he said "Please forgive me." I was not sure what he was referring to, so I asked him "for what?" waiting for his answer. I restated my question, and waited again. He just sat with quivering lip. I don't know if he could not speak, or if the thought was too tender. After a very long wait, I said to him "Honey, you and I have been forgiving each other for almost 65 years, so why would I stop now? Whatever is burdening your mind, I forgive you."

Keith's care at the Aurora Care Center included Hospice staff, as well. Our family watched him closely, also. Though he could not speak, the Staff showed us how to read his expression that would indicate if his pain was increasing. We were then to ask the staff for more medicine. They showed us to watch the bottoms of his feet as skin changed, as well as watching that no bed sores show up. My desire was to feed him whatever he could swallow. Hospice taught me that when the body shuts down, food is repulsive, and actually cruel to lengthen this process. While he didn't drink fluids, he sometimes would take the soaked sponge tabs to moisten his mouth. Other times, he refused. We were careful to remember to always talk encouraging things to him, not knowing if his ears could hear. I told him often, it was alright for him to go on Home. I would be coming later. His breathing had slowed. Three of us had stayed overnight. Most of our family was around him when his breathing stopped. One breath was earthly air and the next was celestial. We called the nurses. Two came and pronounced him gone.

Sadness prevailed as our three children and I proceeded to make arrangements for his memorial at First Baptist Church in Marionville. I realize there are those who choose to have no funeral or memorial of any kind, not even a graveside service. Recently two of my close friends have died, and this was the method chosen for them. However, for me, the memories of this time are indelible deep in my heart that I treasure. It was almost a taste of Heaven—that gathering of family and dear friends, triumphant music, Scripture that ministered comfort to us all, and some sprinkling of humorous remembering as well as wonderful food lovingly offered. Many saw to each detail so the entire church service was without a flaw. Previously, we had a "family only" at the Funeral Home with an open casket. It was at this time that we got to say our "see you later" to this one who meant a lot to us. The internment was in the V.A. Cemetery south of Springfield. After singing "Great

Is Thy Faithfulness" our Pastor again had words of comfort. Limited veteran honors were given, playing of taps, and then the presentation of the flag was given to me that had draped over his casket. I display it in the shadow box given by my family.

The cemetery provides the headstone for each veteran. Keith's name, birth/death and military service dates are etched on it. My internment, when the time comes, can be in the same location, with my information given on the back of the stone. Other etchings that I chose for his were to have a cross at the top and a message below. There can be two lines of 15 characters each line (including spaces). I was given several days to fill the order for my choices. This was more difficult than it might seem, especially the brevity of it. I had been leafing through Keith's Bible, and noticed various verses he had underlined that were special to him. One was Isaiah 41:10. "So do not fear, for I am with you; do not be dismayed, for I am your God. I will strengthen you and help you; I will uphold you with my righteous right hand." (NIV) Trust me—that exceeds the space limit! This condensed form is what I ordered, and they etched it exactly: GOD IS MY GOD (top line) HE UPHOLDS ME. (2nd line).

My New Title

My children and grandchildren showered me with love, visits, phone calls, e-mails and attention in general. What an immeasurable blessing and a help to me! This did not change the fact that I am now a widow. That word had been a description of someone else, but now had to be entered into my present vocabulary. The challenge of changes, day by day.

For instance, the day after Keith's memorial service, our oldest daughter and I attended our Sunday morning church service—with tender hearts, I might say. When the Pastor began to pray, I instinctively reached for Keith's hand to "agree in prayer", as our custom was, at home and in Church. Tears surfaced. It was a long time before I could break that habit. A few Sundays later, as I was feasting on the comfort of fellowship with others, we joined the choir in singing that wonderful song "Will your anchor hold in the storms of life?" This released a flood of tears as countless memories rushed upon me. Memories of times when friends or even medical staff would offer words of sorrow to Keith that he was going through this. His response literally dozens of times was "But I have an Anchor." Jesus, his very present Anchor, was steadying him in those uncharted waters. That phrase is forever indelibly printed on my heart thanks to Keith's words of certainty. As I attempted to reign in my emotions, I considered exiting the Church service, but did regain control. I have learned emotions are very unpredictable.

I would say that one "never gets over it", a comment sometimes made by those who have not experienced the death of a spouse. For instance there is an acquaintance of mine who has a habit of whistling as he works. That sound strikes an instant chord of pleasant memories. Keith whistled often as he worked, hardly realizing it. Occasionally I see someone walking with same build, same frame and even the same limp as Keith had. I immediately want to catch up with him—I have so much I want to tell him. These are just some of the things that make for sad/glad memories.

In all my life, I had not lived alone. After my parents' home, Keith and I were together. I wondered if I would now be fearful, wakeful, disturbed, or how would I react. Of course, there were waves of grief sometimes. But I recalled verses in the Bible I had known for years. However now when it's the Lord and me on this new journey, many verses, actually promises, became "mine", so to speak. For instance: Isaiah 12:2 states "I will trust and not be afraid; for the Lord Jehovah is my strength and my song" . . . . (KJV). He doesn't settle for only removing fear, He gave me a song.

I cannot explain this I can only tell you it is true. The giant step of living alone. I did not *endure* living alone or even *adjust* to living alone. I am <u>content</u> to live alone never once being afraid, wakeful or disturbed. My only explanation is this has been a gift from the One who cared so much for His widowed Mother, as he hung on the cross to ask his disciple John to care for her. I have been blessed from my "day one" to experience peace and contentment. I *know* it is from the Lord.

You widows know how day after day, each of us has to pick up various duties our partners had been handling. I would guess our life routine was not much different from yours—each of us just fitting into the duties that best fit us. In our early years of marriage, Keith did the bookwork of handling bills and banking. It soon became evident that this was easier for me than for him. All the aspects of our financing were discussed and agreed upon together, but the details of the record keeping were done by me. So there was no change for me now in my new role. Driving was a different story. I had driven since I was 16, and driven tractors before that. But Keith enjoyed driving. I really did not. So we just settled into the routine of him doing the driving. I remember being cautioned about that practice, and realized I should have listened. I have found it difficult to become *the* driver, but have had assistance from family and friends, and have relied on a promise found in Psalm 46:1 & 2A—"God is our refuge and strength, a very present help in trouble. Therefore we will not fear." I have found Him to be a present help in many other activities, as well.

It is logical to think that two people who have lived closely together in work and in play, in love and sometimes discord know everything there is to know about the other. Keith and I discovered that this is only partially true. He used to express surprise occasionally to learn something about me he had not known. And I to him. Since his earthly journey has ended I continue to learn about him. I enjoy using his Bible. Some things are underlined, notations or an attached clipping. These are like windows into his soul I had not known before. A particular notation is written by him in the front of his Bible. "I can't. He can. Let Him." No one in our family, including me, had seen that before or had any knowledge that prompted his recording it. We thought it worthy of being printed on the power point screen during Keith's memorial.

Repeat—Can Two Walk Together?

Keith and I certainly do not consider that we had all the answers to such an important question. Our efforts sometimes worked and sometimes did not. Stumbling was followed by trying again. Never did a disagreement ever include an option to call it quits. It was not part of our vocabulary. The second part of Amos 3:3 has to be included in the answer—"Except they be agreed". To start any marriage, II Corinthians 6:14 states that a "believer should not be yoked together with an unbeliever." There are numerous choices made every day that need to be agreed upon. A team with one pulling one way and the other pulling the other way cannot last. We found it necessary to agree on finances, each choice of land we invested in, our homes and other purchases, as well. Both opinions were always considered in this and other decisions.

I was very grateful that when some of Keith's final care required a choice as to radiation treatments, Hospice involvement, and nursing home care that he was coherent enough in each case to voice his agreement. I did not want to make such weighty decisions by myself.

I know we made mistakes as we raised our children. That fact could be easily confirmed by asking them. I also know and have found this to be true over and over that the Lord IS a very present help. Without His help, we would have failed for sure. We are so grateful that each one of our children has chosen a mate who pulls together with them. And grateful that each has remained married for a long time, not because it has been easy, but because of their goal.

If we rely on current trends, we might set marriage aside by living together without a commitment. Or, we might enter marriage with an attitude of a trial run such as "if it doesn't work out we can call it quits." But if we want God's plan for marriage, it is important to consider His question. "Can two walk together?" Statistics and present customs would say "No, hardly ever." But God gives a choice: "<u>except</u> they be agreed." That puts the sovereign Lord in control of each daily situation, helping us, leading us. When both partners choose <u>His</u> plan, He does not necessarily offer *easy,* but does offer *rewarding.*